WILLIAM MURFREE
TAX RECEIPT BOOK

❧❧

HERTFORD COUNTY
NORTH CAROLINA

- 1768-1770 -

Copied by:

Raymonf Parker Fouts

Southern Historical Press, Inc.
Greenville, South Carolina

This volume was reproduced
from a personal copy located in
the Publishers private library

Please direct all correspondence and book orders to:
SOUTHERN HISTORICAL PRESS, Inc.
PO Box 1267
Greenville, SC   29602-1267

Originally printed: Cocoa, FL 1993
Copyright 1993 by: Raymond Parker Fouts
Copyright Transferred 2023 to:
        Southern Historical Press, Inc.
ISBN #978-1-63914-173-9
Printed in the United States of America

These records were made available on microfilm [Reel #P. 291] by the kindness of George Stevenson, Private Manuscripts Archivist, North Carolina Department of Cultural Resources, Division of Archives and History, Raleigh, North Carolina.

The following information appears on the Private Collections Work Sheet:

> "Acquisition Information: Received as a gift from the Tennessee State Library and Archives, Nashville, on February 5, 1992; accessioned on March 19, 1992.
> History and Description: This volume appears to be a private record kept by William Murfree, sheriff of Hertford County, as a result of an investigation into the public accounts by the General Assembly of 1768 which reported that many of the county sheriffs were in arrears in their settlements with the colonial treasury. Murfree seems to have kept this record to show precisely what had been collected in his name and from whom. He not only names the taxpayers of the county, but indicates which of the three years they were subject to pay tax in the county, the sum collected, and, frequently, to whom they had paid the tax and the medium of exchange."

These records are a valuable source for researchers in Bertie, Chowan, Gates and Northampton Counties, as well as those in the "burned" county of Hertford.

Each original page in this small volume is written on both left and right-hand leaves. The written matter on each has been typed on one page, with approximately four blank spaces dividing the two leaves. All surnames have been typed in capitals.

"Junr" denotes a underlined letter/word. "Rec/d/" denotes a interlined letter. "Jun/r/" denotes both underlined and interlined. "lested" denotes underlining to emphasize verbatim transcription. "Stephen" denotes a crossed-out word. "=====" denotes a word both crossed-out and illegible. "___" denotes a letter/word missing. Entries are divided by full width "------." The end of each original page is denoted by full width "======."

Each original page has been assigned a number, within parentheses. The index refers to these assigned numbers. The page number of the original record appears to the right of the assigned number. Female given names are indexed, as are holders of the office of Constable. All names have been indexed, including those crossed-out but still legible. Non-white persons are indexed under "Mixed Blood," or "Mulattoes," the terms used within these records.

TABLE OF CONTENTS

WILLIAM MURFREE TAX RECEIPT BOOK

HERTFORD COUNTY, NORTH CAROLINA

1768-1770

[A]

ARCHERBaker 11
ARNELL Edward 22
ARABA John 37
ALLEN Joshua 38
ARLINE James 39
ARLINE John 39
ALPHIN John 65
ASKEW Josiah 65
ALEXANDER Jn/o/..... 76
ARCHER Jacob 84
ARCHER Jacob 87
ASKEW James 88
ANDREWS Rich/d/..... 108
ARCHER Tho/s/....... 125
ALLEN Wm 133
ASKEW Wm 140
ARCHER Marry 147
ASKEW Nicholas 148

[B]

BISHOP Mason 99
BRITT Nathan 100
BEAMON Ozias 101
BAKER Richard 104
BRIGERS Robert 105
BAKER Richard 106
BROWN Samuel 113
BROWN Samuel 115
BURRISH Sam/1/. 117
BAKER Thomas 121
BETHIA Trussay 121
BARNS Thomas 122
BRITT Thomas Senr . 123
BOWSER Tho/s/....... 124
BROWN Tho/s/........ 126
BOULTON Tho/s/...... 126
BIRD Tho/s/......... 126
BOYCE Wm. 133
BARNS Wm. 135
BOON Wm 135

BIRD Wm.. S/r/...... 137
BARDEN Wm 142
BALEY Wm. 143
BLAKE Walter 143
BRITT Wm. 144
BIRD Wm. Jur 145
BROWN Wm 146
BAKER Zadock 146
BECK Matthew 148
BOON Nick?olas 148
BUTLER Absalom 3
BLICHENDEN Ab/m/. .. 4
BLANSHARD Amal. 6
BAKER Benj/n/.. Jun/r/ 9
BELCH Benj/n/....... 9
BROWN Benj/n/. Jur.. 9
BROWN Benj/n/. Cont. 11
BARNS Charles 13
BARNS Demsey 17
BARNS Demsey 18
BIZELL David 19
BAKER Daniel 20
BURRUSS Demsey 20
BENTON Elijah 22
BEAMON Edmund 24
BENSON Ezekiel 25
BONIFENT Eliz/a/ ... 27
BRINKLEY Francis ... 27
BROWN Francis 27
BAKER Henry Esqr ... 31
BYRAM Henry 32
BARNS Henry 33
BRADDY James 35
BROWN James 36
BETHAY John 39
BOYCE John 39
BETHAY Jesse 40
BENTON John 41
BOON Jas. Blood 55
BETHEA John 56
BROWN Jesse 59
BOYCE John 60

BIRD Jonas 61
BAKER Joshua 68
BAKER John Esqr 68
BOON James Esqr 69
BURRUSS James 70
BURRUSS Joshua 70
BAKER Jas. Const ... 70
BYRAM James 71
BAKER Jn/o/..Killum 71
BOON John 75
BIRD John 77
BEAMAN John 78
BELCH James 79
BREWER John 81
BRITT James 82
BISHOP John 83
BROWN John Jun/r/ .. 85
BURKETT Josiah 85
BROWN Jane 85
BROWN Josiah 86
BROWN Jn/o/ Col/o/.. 87
BAKER Lawrence 91
BRADDY Lewis 91
BOYCE Mosses Jun/r/. 94
BOYCE Mosses 94
BRICKELL Matth/s/... 98

[C]

CARTER Alex/n/. 2
CARTER Ann 2
COTTON Arth/r/. 7
CRICHELOW Branker .. 10
COTTON Cyrus 14
CRICHELOW Carm/l/ .. 14
CRISTAIN Danl. 18
COTFIELD Edward 26
CAMPBELL John 36
COSTEN James 41
CARTER John 45
CASE Jeremi/ah/.. .. 55
CONE Mc. John 56

1

5

```
(1)  1  Arthur WILLEY          Dr.
1768     To 3 Taxes @ 9/10/d/ .  1  9  6
1769     To 3 Do .. @ 10/6/d/ .  1 11  6
1770     To 2 Do .. @ 7/4 .....   ..14  8
                                 3 15  8         By Procl .......... 3 15  8
----------------------------------------------------------------------------------
         Andrew MATTHEWS
1768     To 2 Taxes @ 9/10 ....  .. 19  8    V    By B. WYNNS Jur. ...   19  8
1769     To 3 Do.. @ 10/6 ....    1 11  6
1770     To 1 Do .. @ 7/4 ....    ..  7  4
                                  2 18  6
----------------------------------------------------------------------------------
        -Amos SMITH             Dr.
17608    To 1 Tax    @ 9/10 ....  ..  9 10
1769     To 2 Do.. @ 10/6 ....    1  1
1770     To 2 Do.. @ 7/4 ....     .. 14  8
                                  2  5  6
----------------------------------------------------------------------------------
         Aaron HARRELL          Dr.
1768     To 2 Taxes @ 9/10        1  1       v.   By By (sic) B. WYNNS Junr  1  1
==================================================================================

(2)  2  -Adria=n SCOTT ......... Dr.
1768     To 1 Tax    @ 7/4 9/10/d/..  9 10
----------------------------------------------------------------------------------
        -Aaron ELLISS .......... Dr.         to be paid by John ELES by Novr
1768     To 1 Tax . @ 9/10 ..... ..  9 10    Court Next
1769     To 1 Do .. @ ==== 10/6  .. 10  6    present L: BAKER
                                  1  0  4    Recd. of John ELES          1 ..  4
----------------------------------------------------------------------------------
        -Aaron MAINER           Dr
1768     To 1 Tax . @ 9/10 ..... ..  9 10    V    By B: WYNNS Junr. .     9 10
1769     To 2 Do .. @ 10/6 .....  .1  1 ..        Recd. by T: vANN        1  1
                                  1 10 10                                 1 10 10
----------------------------------------------------------------------------------
         Alexander CARTER       Dr.
1768     To 3 Taxes @ 9/10 .....  1  9  6
----------------------------------------------------------------------------------
        -Abraham SCOTT ......... Dr
1768     To 2 Taxes @ 9/10 ..... .. 19  8
----------------------------------------------------------------------------------
         Ann CARTER ........... Dr
1769     To 3 Taxes @ 10/6 .....  1 11  6
1770     To 4 Do .. @ 7/4 ......  1  9  4
                                  3  0 10
==================================================================================

(3)  3  -Absalom BUTLER         Dr
1769     To 1 Tax . @ 10/6 ..... .. 10  6
1770     To 1 Do .. @ 7/4 ......  ..  7  4
                                    17 10     Recd ....................  17 10
----------------------------------------------------------------------------------
        -Anthony MATTHEWS       Dr
1770     To 2 Taxes @ 7/4  ..... .. 14  8     Rec/d/ ...................  14  8
----------------------------------------------------------------------------------
```

(3) (Cont.) -Aaron ODOM   Dr.
1770   To 1 Tax . @ 7/4 .... 7 4   Rec/d/. 7 4

        -Asa GWIN   Dr.
1770   To 1 Tax . @ 7/4 .... 7 4

        Abraham PORTER
1768   To 6 Taxes @ 9/10 ..... 2 19 -   1768
1769   To 6 Do .. @ 10/6 ..... . 3 3 -   1769 Rec/d/. .... 7 4 --
1770   To 3 Do. . @ 7/4 ..... 1 2   1770
                                7 4 0

        -Ann SANDEFER   Dr.
1768   To 2 Taxes @ 9/10 .... 19 8   Rec/d/. in part 1 13
1770   To 2 Do .. @ 7/4 .... 14 8   Rec/d/. in full 1 4
                                1 14 4   1 14 4
===
(4) 4 Absalom HOLLAWAY
1768   To 3 Taxes @ 9/10 ..... 1 9 6   By prol? 1 9 6

        Aaron HINTON .... Dr
1768   To 1 Tax . @ 9/10 .... 9 10

        -Absalom RALLS .... Dr.
1768   To 2 Taxes @ 7/4 9/10 .. .. 19 8
1769   To 1 Do. . @ 10/6 .... 10 6
1770   To 1 Do .. @ 7/4 .... 7 4
                                1 17 6

        Abraha/m/. BLICHENDEN
==1768 To 2 Taxes @ 9/10 .... 19 8
1769   To 1 Do .. @ 10/6 .... 10 6
1770   To 1 Do .. @ 7/4 .... .7 4
                                1 4? 6

                (blank)
===
(5) 5 Amos HINTON .... Dr
1768   To 2 Takes @ 9/10 .... 19 =8
1769   To 2 Do .. @ 10/6 ..... 1 1
                                2 0 8

        Absalom RALLS .... Dr.
1768   To 1 Tax   @ 9/10 .....   9 10

        -Absalom FLUDD   Dr.
1768   To 2 Taxes @ 9/10 .....   19 8
1770   To 2 Do .. @ 7/4 .... 14 8   By prol 1 14 4
                                1 14 4   Cost 2/8 Rec/d/

        Abel MANLEY .... Dr.
1768   To 5 Taxes @ 9/10 ..... 2 9 2
1769   To 5 Do .. @ 10/6 ..... 2 12 6

(5) (Cont.)   5 1 8

        Agness DAWS .... Dr.
1768   To 2 Taxes @ 9/10/d/... .. 19 8
1769   To 2 Do .. @ 10/6 ..... 1 1
1770   To 1 Do .. @ 7/4 .....   7 4
                                2..8 -   Rec/d/. by Colo. WYNNS   2 8
===

(6) 6 -Aaron SOWELL   Dr.
1768   To 1 Tax . @ 9/10 .... 9 10
1769   To 2 Do .. @ 10/6 ..... 1 1
1770   To 1 Do .. @ 7/4 .... 7 4
                                1 18 2

        -Arthur DOUGALL   Dr.
1768   To 1 Tax . @ 9/10 .... 9 10

        Amariah BLANSHARD
1768   To 7 Taxes @ 9/10 ..... 3 8 10   By prol 3 8 10
1770   To 8 Do .. @ 7/4 ..... 2 18 8   1770 By Procl 2 18 8
                                6 7 6   76 7 6

        -Ann WATSFORD   Dr
1768   To 2 Taxes @ 9/10 .....   19 8

        -Absalom HALL .... Dr.
1768   To 1 Tax @ 9/10 .... 9 10   BW   By B. WYNNS Jur.   9 10
1769   To 1 Do .. @ 10/6 .... 10 6 69   By Proc 10 6
1770   To 1 Do. . @ 7/4 .... 7 4   70   By do 7 4
                                1 7 8   1 7 8
===

(7) 7 Adam HARRELL   Dr
1768   To 1 Tax @ 9/10 .... 9 10
1769   To 1 Do .. @ 10/6 .... 10 6
1770   To 1 Do .. @ 7/4 .... 7 4
                                1 7 8

        -Amy WORRELL .... Dr.
1769   To 2 Taxes @ 10/6 ..... 1 1   By Procl 1 1

        Arthur COTTON .... Dr
1769   To 6 Taxes @ 10/6 .... 3 3

        Ann THORN .... Dr
1770   To 2 Taxes @ 7/4 .... 14 8   Rec/d/ 14 8

        -Alexander LEVEY   Dr.
1770   To 1 Tax . @ 7/4   .. 7 4   1770 By Procl 7 4

        -Amos FREEMAN .... Dr
1770   To 4 Taxes @ 7/4 ..... 1 9 4

        Abram JONES .... Dr

9

(7) (Cont.)
```
1770    To 6 Taxes @ 7/4 .....   2  4              1770  By Procl ...........   2  4
```
==

(8) 8 -Aaron HOLLAMON   Dr.
```
1770    To 1 Tax . @ 7/4 .....   ..  7  4                By Procl ...........     7  4
```

Ann VANPELT .... Dr.
```
1770    To 9 Taxes @ 7/4 .....   3  6                    By Procl ...........   2 18  8
```

Benton MOORE .... Dr.   1768
```
1768    To 4 Taxes @ 9/10 .....  1 19  4          69
1769    To 4 Do .. @ 10/6 .....  2  2  -          70  By Procl. ..........   5 10  8
1770    To 4 Do .. @ 7/4 ......  1  9  4
                                 5 10  8
```

-Benjamin FENDLEY
```
1768    To 1 Tax . @ 9/10/d/ .. ..  9 10
```

-Barneby GODWIN   Dr
```
1768    To 1 Tax . @ 9/10 .....    9 10
1769    To 2 Do .. @ 10/6 .....  1  1
                                 1 10 10
```

-Benjamin MORRISS   Dr
```
1768    To 1 Tax ....(sic).....  ..  9 10
1769    To 1 Do ...............  .. 10  6
                                 1  0  4
```
==

(9) 9 Benjamin WYNNS   Dr
```
        To 21 Taxes @ 9/10 .... 10  6  6
1768    1 Chair with 2 wheels . 1 -----            Rec/d/ ............. 33 19 10
1769    To 24 Taxes @ 10/6      12 12
        1 Chair with 2 wheels . 1
1770    To 22 Taxes @ 7/4 .....  8  1  4
                                33 19 10
```

-Benj/n/. BAKER Jun/r/   Dr.
```
1768    To 2 Taxes @ 9/10 .....  .. 19  8
1769    To Search? @ 10/6 ..... (blank)
1770    To 1 Tax . @ 7/4 ......  ..  7  4          By Procl ..........   1  7  -
                                 1  7  -
```

-Benjamin BELCH   Dr
```
1768    To 1 Tax ..............  ..  9 10
1770    To 1 Do ..............   ..  7  4
                                17  2              By Proc ............   17  2
```

Benjamin BROWN Jun/r/.
```
1768    To 2 Takes @ 9/10/d/ .. .. 19  8
1769    To 1 Do Search ........  .. 10  6
1770    To 4 Do .. @ 7/4 ......  .1  9  4          1770  By Procl. ..........   1  9  4
                                 2 19  6
```
==

```
(10) 10 Benjamin SUMNER
1769    To 5 Taxes @ 10/6 .....  2 12  6
1770    To 3 Do .. @ 7/4 ......  1  2
                                 3 14  6          By Colo. SUMNER      3 14  6
---------------------------------------------------------------------------------
1770    Benjamin WEEKS        Dr.
1769    To 2 Taxes @ 7/4 .....  .. 14  8          By prol ...........   14  8
---------------------------------------------------------------------------------
        -Benjamin TOMSON
1769    To 1 Tax .............  .. 10  6
---------------------------------------------------------------------------------
        Branker CRICHLOW Patr.
1769    To 3 Taxes @ 7/4 10/6   1 11  6           By Wm.. MABRY ......  1  2  6
1770    To 1 Do ..............  --  7  4          By prol. ...........  . 16  4
                                1 18 10                                1 18 10
---------------------------------------------------------------------------------
        Benjamin WILLIAMSON       10 (sic)
1769    To 7 Taxes @ 10/6 .....  3 13  6          By prol ...........  5 -- --
1770    To 6 Do .. @ 7/4 ......  2  4             By prol               17  6
                                 5 17  6                                5 17  6
---------------------------------------------------------------------------------
        -Benjamin NORVILLE    Dr
1769    To 2 Taxes @ 10/6 .....  1  1             By Procl ..........  1 15  8
1770    To 2 Do .. @ 7/4 ......  .. 14  8
                                 1 15  8
=================================================================================

(11) 11-Benjamin EARLY        Dr.
1770    To 1 Tax .............  .  7  4           Rec/d/ ............   7  4
---------------------------------------------------------------------------------
        -Baker ARCHER         Dr.
1770    To 3 Taxes @ 7/4 .....  1  2
---------------------------------------------------------------------------------
        -Barneby HOBBS        Dr.
1770    To 2 Taxes @ 7/4 .....  .. 14  8
---------------------------------------------------------------------------------
        -Benjamin DAWS        Dr
1770    To 1 Tax . @ 7/4 .....  ..  7  4
---------------------------------------------------------------------------------
        Benjamin BROWN Cont.
1770    To 2 Taxes @ 7/4 .....  .. 14  8          By Procl ..........   14  8
---------------------------------------------------------------------------------
        -Caleb POLSON ........ Dr
1768    To 2 Taxes @ 9/10 ....  .. 19  8
1769    To 2 Do .. @ 10/6 ....  1 21
1770    To 2 Do .. @ 7/4 .....  .. 14  8
                                2 15  4
---------------------------------------------------------------------------------
        -Charles EURE ........ Dr
1768    To 3 Taxes @ 9/10 ....  1  9  6    V.     By B: WYNNS Junr ...  1  9  6
1769    To 2 Do .. @ 10/6       1 21              Rec/d/. ...........   1 15  8
1770    To 22 (sic) Do @ 7/4 .  .. 14  8                                3  5  2
                                3 =5  2
=================================================================================
```

```
(12) 12-Charles HARRELL        Dr
1768    To 1 Tax ..co? .......  ..  9 10
1769    To 1 Do .............   .. 10  6
1770    To 1 Do .............   ..  7  4
                                   1  7  8
------------------------------------------------------------------------
        Christopher RIDDICK
1769    To 3 Taxes @ 10/6 ....  1 11  6
1770    To 4 Do .. @ 7/4 .....  1  9  4
                                3  0 10
------------------------------------------------------------------------
        -Charity EURE          Dr
1769    To 1 Tax .............  .. 10  6
1770    To 1 Do .............   ..  7  4      V.   Rec/d/ ............     17 10
                                  17 10
------------------------------------------------------------------------
        Charles SANDERS        Dr
1769    To 1 Tax .............  .. 10  6             By B: WYNNS Junr ... .. 10  6
------------------------------------------------------------------------
        Charles HEDGSPETH      Dr
1769    To 1 Tax .............  ..' 10  6            By Capt BAKER ......  . 17 10
1770    To 1 Do .............   ..  7  4
                                  17 10
========================================================================
(13) 13 Charles RUSSELL        Dr.
1769    To 1 Tax .............  .. 10  6
1770    To 1 Do .............   ..  7  4
                                  17 10            Rec/d/. ............     17 10
------------------------------------------------------------------------
        -Charles VANN ........ Dr.
1769    To 1 Tax .............  .. 10  6
1770    To 1 Do .............   ..  7  4
                                  17 10
------------------------------------------------------------------------
        Charles BARNS          Dr.
1768    To 1 Tax .............     9 10           By Procl. .......... (blot) 8/d/
1769    To 1 Do .............   .. 10  6          By prol ............  1  1 ..
1770    To 1 Do .............   ..  7  4                                 1  7  8
                                1  7  8
------------------------------------------------------------------------
        Christopher SUMPTURE (sic)
1768    To 1 Tax .............          ..  9 10
17769   To 1 Do .............          .. 10  6
1770    To 1 Do .............              ..  7  4
        Geo. LITTLE is to pay the above 1  7  8
------------------------------------------------------------------------
        -Charles JONES ........ Dr.
1768    To 1 Tax .............  ..  9 10
1770    To 1 Do .............   ..  7  4
                                  17  2
========================================================================
(14) 14-Cyrus COTTON ......... Dr.
1768    To 2 Taxes @ 9/10 ....  .. 19  8
```

(14) (Cont.)
```
         -Carter NICKENS ....... Dr
1768    To 1 Tax .............        9 10
1769    To 1 Do .............. .. 10  6          By prol ............ 1 15
1770    To 2 Do .. @ 7/4 ..... .. 14  8
                                  1 15 -
```

```
         -Cullens SESSUMS ...... Dr
1768    To 4 Takes @ 9/10 ....  1 19  4
1769    To 3 Do .. @ 10/6 ....  1 11  6
1770    To 2 Do .. @ 7/4 ..... .. 14  8
                                 4  5  6
```

```
         -Charles WEVER ........ Dr.
1768    To 2 Taxes @ 9/10 .... .. 19  8
1769    To 2 Do .. @ 10/6 ....  1  1
1770    To 2 Do .. @ 7/4 ..... .. 14  8
                                 2 15  4
```

```
         -Carmichael Crichelow
1769    To 3 Taxes @ 10/6 ....  1 11  6         Rec/d/ in part ..... 2 -  -
1770    To 1 Do .............. ..  7  4         By prol ............ . 11 4
                                 1 18 10                             2 11 4
1768    To 1 Do ..............     9 10
        Cost of worrant 2/8      2  8  8
```
==
```
(15) 15 Charles SKINNER
1770    To 23 Taxes @ 7/4 ....  8  8  8         By Procl ........... 8 8 8
```

```
        Charles JENKINS Jun/r/.
1770    To 3 Taxes @ 7/4 .....  1  2            By prol ............ 1 2
```

```
        Christopher MARTIN
1770    To 1 Tax ............. ..  7  4
```

```
        Cader POWELL ......... Dr.
1769    To 6 Taxes @ 10/6 ....  3  3            By Procl .......... 3..3 --
1770    To 6 Do. . @ 7/4 .....  2  4    1770    By Prockl. ........ 2 4 --
                                 5  7                                5 7
```

```
        Charles WILDER ....... Dr
1770    To 1 Tax ............. ..  7  4
```

```
        Culmeer? SESSUMS      Dr.
1770    To 4? Taxes @ 7/4 .....  1  9  4
```
==
```
(16) 16-Daniel PARKER         Dr.
1768    To 3 Taxes @ 9/10 .....  1  9  6    BW  By B. WYNNS ........ 1 9 6
```

```
        Colo. Demsey SUMNER
1768    To 4 Taxes @ 9/10 .....  1 19  4
```

```
        -Demsey ROOKS ........ Dr.
```

(16) (Cont.)
```
1768    To 2 Taxes @ 9/10 ....  .. 19  8
1769    To 2 Do .. @ 10/6 ....  .1  1
1770    To 1 Do Const. .......  ..  7  4        By Procl ..........  2  8  -
        To Const. fees 2/8      2  8            By Constable fee ...     2 ˙8
```

```
        -David UMFLEET ........  Dr
1768    To 1 Tax .............  ..  9 10        V ... By B. WYNNS Jur. ...     9 10
1770    To 1 Do .............   ..  7  4        By Procl ..........     7  4
1769    To 1 Do .............   .. 10  6
                                1 =7? 8
```

```
        Daniel ROGERS ........  Dr.
1768    To 1 Tax .............  ..  9 10        V   By B. WYNNS Jur. ...  1  1? 4
1769    To 1 Do .............   .. 10  6        V.  Rec/d/ of E. COPLAND
                                1  0  4             not Sartain Listed    7  4
```
==
```
(17) 17-David SMITH          Dr.
1768    To 2 Taxes @ 9/10 ....  .. 19  4 8
1769    To 2 Do .. @ 10/6 ....  1  1
1770    To 1 Do .............   ..  7  4
                                2  8 0 0
```

```
        -Demsey SUMNER          Dr.
1768    To 1 Tax .............  ..  9 10
1769    To 1 Do .............   .. 10  6
1770    To 1 Do .............   ..  7  4
                                1  7  8
```

```
        -Danl. ROGERS of Robt.
17698   To 2 Taxes @ 9/10 ....  .. 19  8        By John HARE .......  1θ9=8
```

```
        -David WATSON .........  Dr.
1768    To 2 Taxes @ 9/10/d/ .  .. 19  8        Rec/d/ .............     19  8
```

```
        -Demsey BARNES          Dr.
17768   To 2 Taxes @ 9/10/d/ .  .. 19  8    BW  Rec/d/ ............  3  -----
1769    To 4 Do .. @ 10/6 ....  2  2            By B. WYNNS Junr. ..    19  8
1770    To 3 Do .. @ 7/4 .....  1  2
                                4  3  8
```
==
```
(18) 18-Demsey VANN ..........  Dr.
1770    To 1 Tax .............  ..  7  4
```

```
        -Demsey ODAM            Dr.
1770    To 3 Taxes @ 7/4 .....  1  2            By Procl ..........  1  2
```

```
        -Demsey WILLIAMS
1770    To 1 Tax .............  ..  7  4
```

```
        -David HARRELL ........  Dr.
1770    To 2 Taxes @ 7/4 .....  .. 14  8        Rec/d/ .............  .. 14  8
```
----

(18) (Cont.)
```
        -Demsey HARRELL          Dr.
1770    To 1 Tax .............  ..  7  4
```

```
        -Demsey BARNES ........  Dr.
1768    To 1 Tax .............  --  9 10
```

```
        -Daniel CHRISTAIN       Dr.
1768    To 1 Tax .............  ..  9 10
```
===
```
(19) 19 Daniel DAVIS .........  Dr.
1768    To 1 Tax .............  ..  9 10        By prol ...........  1  7  8
1769    To 1 Do ..............  .. 10  6
1770    To 1 Do ..............  ..  7  4
                                   1  7  8
```

```
        David HORTON .........  Dr.
1768    To 1 Tax .............  --  9 10
```

```
        -David HANCOCK ........  Dr.
1768    To 1 Tax .............  ..  9 10
1769    To 1 Do ..............  .. 10  6
1770    To 1 Do ..............  ..  7  4
                                   1  7  8        Rec/d/ ............  1  7  8
```

```
        -Demsey MAUDLING        Dr
1768    To 1 Tax .............  ..  9 10
1769    To 1 Do ..............  .. 10  6
                                   1  0  4
```

```
        -David BIZELL .........  Dr.
1768    To 2 Taxes @ 9/10/d/ .  .. 19  8
1769    To 2 Do .. @ 10/6 ....  1  1
1770    To 2 Do .. @ 7/4 .....  .. 14  8
                                   2 15  4        Rec/d/ ............  2 15  4
```
===
```
(20) 20 Daniel DEANES           Dr.
1768    To 5 Taxes @ 9/10 ....  2  9  2
1770    To 3 Do .. @ 7/4 .....  1  2
                                   3 11  2        Rec/d/. ...........  3 11  2
```

```
176     -Daniel BAKER .........  Dr
176=8   To 1 Tax .............      9 10
```

```
        -David VOLLENTINE
1768    To 2 Taxes @ 9/10 ....  .. 19  8
1769    To 2 Do .. @ 10/6 ....  1  1            By Procl ..........  2  8 --
1770    To 1 Do ..............  ..  7  4
                                   2  8
```

```
        -Demsey BURRUSS         Dr.
1768    To 1 Tax ... 9/10/d/ .  ..  9 10        By Procl ..........  1  0  4
1769    To 1 Do ..............  .. 10  6
                                   1  0  4
```

(20) (Cont.)
```
          Demsey WOOD ..........                              By Procl ........... 1 11 10
1768      To 1 Tax .............        9 10
1770      To 3 Do. .............       .1  2
                                        1 11 10
```
===

```
(21) 21-David SANDERS
1770      To 1 Tax .............   ..  7  4
1769      To 1 Do ..............   .. 10  6
              & Cost                  17 10
```

```
          Demsey KNIGHT
1769      To .1 Tax ............       10  6
1770      To 1 Do ..............   ..  7  4
                                      17 10               By prol ............ . 17 10
```

```
          Day RIDLEY
1770      To 5 Taxes @ 7/4 .....   1 16  8       1770  By Procl ........... 1 16  8
```

```
          David FORSETT
1770      To 2 Taxes @ 7/4 .....  .. 14  8             Rec/d/ ............. .. 14  8
```

```
          -Daniel PEELE .........
1770      To 2 Taxes @ 7/4 .....  .. 14  8
```

```
          -Demsey NOWELL
1770      To 1 Tax .............  ..  7  4             By Procl ........... ..  7  4
```
===

```
(22) 22 Elisha PARKER
1768      To 4 Taxes @ 9/10 ....  .1 19  4
1769      To 4 Do .... 10/6 ....   2  2
1770      To 4 Do .... 7/4 .....  .1  9  4
                                   5 10  8       By Pro Colo. D SUMNER 5 10  8
```

```
          -Elizabeth RIDDICK
1768      To 6 Taxes @ 9/10 ....   2 19      BW   By B. WYNNS Jur .... 2 19
```

```
          -Elijah BENTON
1768      To 2 Taxes @ 9/10/d/ .  .. 19  8
1769      To 2 Do .. @ 10/6 ....  .1  1
1770      To 2 Do .. @ 7/4 .....  .. 14  8
                                   2 15  4
```

```
          -Edward ARNELL
1768      To 2 Taxes @ 9/10 ....  .. 19  8      BW   By B: WYNNS Jur. ...   19  8
```

```
          -Elizabeth LINCH
1768      To 2 Taxes @ 9/10 ....  .. 19 48            Rec/d/. ............ 1  6  8
1769      To 1 Do ..............  .. 10  6
17670     To 1 Do ..............  ..  7  4
                                   1 17 20?
```
===

```
(23) 23 Edward WARREN
1768    To 5 Taxes @ 9/10 ....   2  9  2
1769    To 3 Do .. @ 10/6 ....  .1 11 76
                                 4  0  8
1770    To 2 Do .. @ 7/4 .....  .. 14  8
                                 4 15  4
```

                    (blank)

```
        -Edward PILENT
1768    To 1 Tax .............  .. 9 10      V    By B. WYNNS Jur ..... .. 9 10
```

```
        Edward WARRIN Junr
1768    To 2 Taxes @ 9/10 ....  .. 19  8     BW   By B. WYNNS Jur. ...  2  0  8
1769    To 2 Do .. @ 10/6 ....   1  1 ..    -BW
                                 2  0  8     1770 By Procl ...........  .. 14  8
                                                                        1  15?6?
```

```
        Edward HARE .........
1768    To 10 Taxes @ 9/10 ...   4 18  4
1769    To 9 Do ... @ 10/6 ...   4 14  6
                                 9 12 10     BW
```

```
        -Edmund PINNINGTON
1768    To 2 Taxes @ 9/10 ....  . 19  8
```
==

```
(24) 24 Esaw DICKERSON
1768    To 1 Tax .............  .. 9 10?
1769    To 1 Do .............   .. 10  6
1770    To 1 Do .............   .. 7  4     Rec/d/. ...........  1  7  8
                                 1  7  8
```

```
        -Edmund HOLLAMON
1768    To 5 Taxes @ 9/10/d/ .  .2  9  2
1769    To 3 Do .. @ 10/6 ....   1  1       Rec/d/. ...........  4  4 10
1770    To 2 Do .. @ 7/4 .....  .. 14  8
                                 4  4 10
```

```
        -Elijah HARROLD
1768    To 1 Tax . @ 9/10/d/ .  .. 9 10
1769    To 1 Do .............   .. 10  6
1770    To 1 Do .............   .. 7  4     Rec/d/ ...........  1  7  8
                                 1  7  8
```

```
        -Edmund BEAMON
1768    To 1 Tax .............  .. 9 10
1769    To 1 Do .............   .. 10  6
                                 1  0  4
```

```
        Ezekiel SLAWSON
1768    To 1 Tax .............  .. 9 10
1769    To 1 Do .............   .. 10  6
1770    To 1 Do .............   .. 7  4
```

==

(25) 25 Emelich P_NNINGTON
1769   To 1 Tax 710 6
1770   To 1 Do 7 4
                                   17 10

        Ezekiel BENSON
1769   To 1 Tax .... 10 6   Rec/d/. .... 1 1/2?

        Elizabeth LEADOM
1769   To 1 Tax 10 6

        Edward GATLING
1769   To 3 Taxes @ 10/6 .... 1 11 6   By Edwd. GATLING Jn/r/. 10 6
1770   To 2 Do .. @ 7/4 .... 14 8   By pro1 .... 1 15 8
                                 2 6 2   2 6 2

        Edward HOWARD
1769   To 1 Tax 10 6
1770   To 1 Do .... 7 4   1770 By Procl. 7 4
                                   17 10

        -Elisha WILSON ....
1769   To 2 Taxes @ 10/6 .... 1 1
1770   To 2 Do .. @ 7/4 .... 14 8
                                 1 15 8

==

(26) 26-Edward COTFIELD
1769   To 1 Tax 10 6

        -Elijah DAWS ....
1769   To 1 Tax 10 6
1770   To 1 Do .... -- 7 4
                                   17 10

        Edward FELL
1769   To 1 Tax .... -- 10 6

        Emelias DARRING
1770   To 5 Taxes @ 7/4 ..... .1 16 8   By. B. F 1 16 8

        Ezekiel DANIŁEL
1770   To 1 Tax .... -- 7 4

        Elijah HOWARD
1770   To 1 Tax .... -- 7 4

        -Epheriam KEEFE
1770   To 1 Tax 7 4

==

(27) 27 Elizabeth BONIFENT

```
(27) (Cont.)
1770    To 7 Taxes @ 7/4 .....  2 11  4              By Gorge (sic) SWOPE  2 11  4
------------------------------------------------------------------------------------
        -Francis DOUGHTIE
1768    To 1 Tax ............. .. 79410
1769    To 1 Do .............. .. 10  6
1770    To 2 Do .............. .. 14  8
                                 1 173 0?
------------------------------------------------------------------------------------
        Francis BRINKLEY
1768    To 2 Taxes @ 9/10 .... .. 19  8      V
1769    To .. Do . @ 10/6 .... .1  1         V.    By B. WYNNS Jur ....  2 -  8
                                 2  0  8
------------------------------------------------------------------------------------
        -Francis SANDERS
1770    To 4 Taxes @ 7/4 .....  1  9  4              Rec/d/ .............  1  9  4
------------------------------------------------------------------------------------
        Francis OSMUNT
1770    To 1 Tax ............. --  7  4
------------------------------------------------------------------------------------
        Francis BROWN
1768    To 2 Taxes @ 9/10 .... .  19  8
1769    To 1 Do 10/6 ......... .. 10  6
1770    To 1 Do .............. ..  7  4
                                 1 17 68?
====================================================================================

(28) 28 Francis RALLS
1770    To 3 Taxes @ 7/4 .....  1  2
------------------------------------------------------------------------------------
        George WILLIAMS
1768    To 1 Tax ............. ..  9 10
  69    To 1 Do .............. .. 10  6
  70    To 2 Do .. @ 7/4 ..... .. 14  8             Rec/d/ .............  1 15
                                 1 15 -
------------------------------------------------------------------------------------
        George WILLIAMS Cons/t/. & Jun/r/.
1768    To 3 Taxes @ 9/10 ....  1  9  6
  69    To 3 Do .. @ 10/6 ....  1 11  6            By Procl ..........  4 10  4
  70    To 4 Do .. @ 7/4 .....  1  9  4
                                 4 10  4
------------------------------------------------------------------------------------
        George PILAND
1768    To 1 Tax ............. --  9 10
  69    To 1 Do .............. -- 10  6
  70    To 1 Do .............. --  7  4            Rec/d/ .............  1  7  8
                                 1  7  8
------------------------------------------------------------------------------------
        George GATLING
1768    To 1 Tax .............     9 10
  69    To 1 Do .............. .. 10  6..    BW    By B: WYNNS Jur ....    10  6
                                 1?  0  4
====================================================================================

(29) 29 George RUSSELL
```

(29) (Cont.)
```
1769    To 1 Tax ..............  .. 10  6
  70    To 1 Do ..............  ..  7  4
                                   17 10
```

George WILLIAMS
```
1770    To 1 Tax ..............  ..  7  4
```

George SCOTT
```
1770    To 1 Tax ..............  ..  7  4
```

George EZELL
```
1768    To 1 Tax ..............  ..  9 10
  69    To 1 Do ..............      10  6
  70    To 1 Do ..............  ..   7  4
                                    1  7  8
```

Grafton IRELAND
```
1769    To 1 Tax ..............  -- 10  6                By Procl ........... .. 17 10
  70    To 1 Do ..............  ..  7  4
                                   17 10
```

George WARD
```
1770    To 1 Tax ............  --  7  4                  Rec/d/. ............ .  7  4
```
==

(30) 30 George LITTLE Esq/r/.
```
1770    To 9 Taxes @ 7/4 .....  3  6          1770  Rec/d/. ............  3  6
```

Gabriel MANLEY
```
1770    To 1 Tax ..............  ..  7  4
```

George POWELL
```
1770    To 5 Taxes @ 7/4 .....  1 16  8      1770  By Procl. p/r/. Son Demsey 1  16 8
```

George EARLY
```
1770    To 1 Tax ..............  ..  7  4
```

Geo/r/.. Paletiah WYNNS
```
1770    To 1 Tax ..............  ..  7  4       -1770  By Procl ........... ..  7  4
```

Henry DILDA
```
1768    To 1 Tax ..............  ..  9 10
1770    To 2 Do ..............  ..   7  4
                                    17  2
```

Henry PRICE
```
1768    To 1 Tax ..............  ..  9 10
  69    To 1 Do ..............  ..  10  6
                                    1  0  4
```
==

(31) 31 Hardy MORGAN
```
1768    To 1 Tax ..............  ..  9 10
  69    To 1 Do ..............  ..  10  6
```

(31) (Cont.)

1 0 4

Henry SMITH
1768   To 2 Taxes @ 9/10/d/ . .. 19 8
1770   To 3 Do .. @ 7/4 ..... .1 2
                                2 1 8
1769   To 2 Do .. @ 10/6 .... 1 1
                                3 2 8

Henry BAKER Esqr.
1768   To 18 Taxes @ 9/10 ... 8 17 2   V. .. By B. WYNNS Ju/r/. . 8 17 2
  69   To 12 Do .. @ 10/6 ... 6 6   By prol. 5 15 6
  70   To 12 . Do @ 7/4 .... 4 8   1770 By 80/8/d/ .... 4 .. 8
                               19 11 2   18 13 4

Henry DILDA & Jun/r/.
1768   To 2 Taxes @ 9/10 .... .. 19 8
  69   To 1 .. Do 10 6
                                1 10 2

Henry GOODMON
1768   To 4 Taxes @ 9/10 .... .1 19 4   V. .. By B. WYNNS Jur. ... 1 19 4
1769   To 3 Do .. @ 10/6 .... 1 11 6
                                3 10 10

===

(32) 32 Henry KING
1768   To 14 Taxes @ 9/10 ... 6 17 8   V.   By Benj. WYNNS Ju/r/. 14 15 2
Esqr.69 To 15 . Do @ ..(sic). 7 17 6   V.
                               14 15 2

Henry KING Jun/r/
1768   To 6 Taxes .... 2 19   V. .. By Benjn. WYNNS Ju/r/. 2 19 ..

Hardy JONES
1769   To 2 Taxes @ 10/6 .... 1 1

Henry WARREN ....
1768   To 1 Tax 9 10
  69   To 1 Do 10 6
  70   To 1 Do .... -- 7 4
                                1 7 8

Henry BYRAM
1768   To 1 Tax 9 10

===

(33) 33 Hugh HORTON
1768   To 2 Taxes @ 9/10 .... .. 19 8
  69   To 4 Do .. @ 10/6 .... 2 2   Rec/d/. 3 1 8
                                3 1 8

Humphry MC SIMONS
1768   To 1 Tax 9 10

21

(33) (Cont.)
```
  69    To 1 Do .............. .. 10  6
                                 1  0  4
```

Henry HILL Esqr
```
1769    To 26 Taxes @ 10/6 ... 13 13        Rec/d/. by Extx. ... 27  4  4
  70    To 31 Do. . @ 7/4 .... 13 11  4
                               27  4  4
```

Henry BARNES
```
1769    To 1 Tax ............. .. 10  6        Rec/d/. ............ .  4 ..
  70    To 1 Do .............. .. 7  4
                                  17 10
```

Hannah GRIFFITH
```
1769    To 4 Taxes @ 10/6 .... 2  2            By prol. ........... 3 11  4
  70    To 4 Do .. @ 7/4 ..... 1  9  4
                               3 11  4
```
===

(34) 34 Henry PARTIN
```
1770    To 2 Taxes @ 7/4 ..... .. 14  8
```

Hatton WALKER
```
1770    To 1 Tax ............. .. 7  4        1770 By Procl ........... .. 7  4
```

Hosea NEWSOM
```
1770    To 2 Taxes @ 7/4 ..... .. 14  8
```

Hamer HOMES
```
1770    To 1 Tax ............. .. 7  4
```

Harmon VANPELT
```
1770    To 2 Taxes @ 7/4 ..... .. 14  8        Rec/d/. ............. 14  8
```

John KITTRELL
```
1768    To 5 Taxes @ 9/10/d/ . 2  9  2    V.   By B: WYNNS Ju/r/ .. 2  9  2
```
===

(35) 35 James BRADDY
```
1768    To 7 Taxes @ 9/10/d/ . 3  8 10    V. .. By B: WYNNS Jur. ... 3  8 10
  69    To 7 Do .. @ 10/6 .... 3 13  6
  70    To 7 Do .. @ 7/4 ..... .2 11  4
                               9 13  8
```

James HAYSE
```
1768    To 2 Taxes @ 9/10 .... .. 19  8    V. .. By B. WYNNS Jur .... .. 19  8
17670   To 2 Do .. @ 7/4 ..... .. 14  8        By Procl. .......... 14  8
                                1 14  4                             1 14  4
```

Jacob HAYSE
```
1768    To 1 Tax ............. .. 9 10    V. .. By B. WYNNS Jur. ... . 9 10
1770    To 2 Do .............. .. 14  8        By Procl. .......... . 14  8
                                1  4  6                             1  4  6
```
----

(35) (Cont.)
        Isaac PARKER
1768   To 1 Tax 79410
==

(36) 36 James PRUDEN
1768   To 1 Tax .... 9 10   V. .. By B: WYNNS Jur. 9 10
1770   To 1 Do .... 7 4   1770 By prol. 7 4
                                17 2   17 2

        James PARKER
1768   To 2 Takes @ @ 9/10/d/ .. 19 8
  69   To 2 Do .. @ 10/6 .... 1 1
  70   To 2 Do .. @ @ 7/4 ... .. 14 8
                                 2 15 4

        James /John/ CAMPBELL
1768   To 1 Tax ....   9 10   V. .. By B. WYNNS Jur. 9 10
  69   To 1 Do 10 6
  70   To 1 Do 7 4
                                 1 7 8

        James BROWN
1768   To 5 Taxes @ 9/10/d/ . 2 9 2   By Procl 3 11 4
  69   To 4 Do .. @ 10/6/d/.. 2 2 -
  70   To 4 Do .. @ 7/4 ..... 1 9 4
                                6 0 6
==

(37) 37 Joseph FIGG
1768   To 3 Taxes @ 9/10/d/ . 1 9 6   V. .. By B. WYNNS Jur. ... 1 9 6
  69   To 3 Do .. @ 10/6 .... 1 11 6   mind inqr (sic)
                                3 1

        John ==== RABY
1768   To 1 Tax .... 9 10   V. .. By B. WYNNS Jur. 9 6
  69   To 1 Do 10 6
  70   To 1 Do 7 4
                                 1 7 8

        John DUKE
1768   To 1 Tax 9 10
  69   To 2 Do .. @ 10/6 .... 1 1
  70   To 2 Do .. @ 7/4 .... 14 8
                                 2 5 6

        Joseph GRIFFIN
1768   To 5 Takes @ 9/10/d/ . 2 9 2
  69   To 5 Do @ 10/6/d/ 2 12 6
  70   To 4 Do @ 7/4 .... 1 9 4
                                6 11
==

(38) 38 John POLSON
1768   To 1 Tax 9 10

23

(38) (Cont.)
```
 69   To 1 Do .............   .. 10  6
 70   To 1 Do .............   ..  7  4
                               1  7  87?
```

Josiah MATTHEWS
```
1768  To 1 Tax ............   ..  9 10          By Wm. VANN's Recpt.     9 10
 69   To 1 Do .............   .. 10  6
 70   To 2 Do...@ 7/4......   .. 14  8          By Procl ........... 1  5  --
                               1 15
```

Jeremiah SPEIGHT
```
1768  To 4 Taxes @ 9/10 ....  1 19  4
 69   To 2 Do .. @ 10/6 ....  1  1
 70   To 2 Do .. @ 7/4 .....  .. 14  8
                              3 15
```

Joshua ALLEN
```
1768  To 1 Tax ............   ..  9 10
 69   To 3 Do .. @ 10/6 ....  1 11  6
 70   To 1 Do .............   ..  7  4
                              2  8  8
```

==

(39) 389 John BETHAY mind
```
1768  To 3 Taxes @ 9/10/d/ .  1  9  6      V. .. By B. WYNNS Jur. ... 1  9  6
 70   To 3 Do .. @ ±07/64 ..  1 == 80      1770 By prol. ........... 1  2  -
                              2 11 =6                                2 11  6
```

James ARLINE
```
1768  To 2 Taxes @ 9/10/d/ .  .. 19  8
 69   To 3 Do .. @ 10/6 ....  1 11  6
 70   To 1 Do .............   ..  7  4
                              2 18  6
```

John ARLINE
```
1768  To 4 Taxes @ 9/10/d/ .  1 19  4
 69   To 4 Do .. @ 10/6 ....  2  2
 70   To 4 Do .. @ 7/4 .....  1  9  4
                              5 10  8
```

John BOYCE
```
1768  To 1 Tax ............   ..  9 10
 69   To 1 Do .............   .. 10  6
                              1  0  4
```

==

(40) 40 John WALTERS
```
1768  To 1 Tax ............   ..  9 10
```

James PILAND
```
17768  To 2 Taxes @ 9/10 ....  1  9  6
  69   To 1 Do .............   -- 10  6
  70   To 2 Do .. @ 7/4 .....  -- 14  8
                               2 14  8
```

(40) (Cont.)
```
        Jonathan WILLIAMS
1768    To 1 Tax ............   -- 9 10
1770    To 2 Do .. @ 7/4 .....  -- 14  8
                                 1  4  6      Rec/d/ ............. 1  4  6
```

```
        Jesse BATHAY
1768    To 3 Taxes @ 9/10/d/ .  1  9  6
  69    To 3 Do .. @ 10/6 ....  .1 11  6
                                 3  1
```

```
        Jemima REED afree Multatoe (sic)
1768    To 1 Tax ............   .. 9 10
  69    To 1 Do .............   .. 10  6
                                 1  0  4
  70    To 1 Do .............      7  4
                                 1  7  8
```
==
```
(41) 41 Isaac WALTERS
1768    To 2 Taxes @ 9/10 ....  .. 19  8
  69    To 2 Do .. @ 10/6 ....   1  1
  70    To 2 Do .. @ 7/4 .....  .. 14  8
                                 2 15  4
```

```
        John BENTON ..........
1768    To 6 Taxes @ 9/10/d/ .  2 19
  69    To 6 Do .. @ 10/6/d/ .  3  3       By prol. ........... 8  6  --
  70    To 6 Do .. @ 7/4 .....  2  4
                                 8  6
```

```
        James COSTEN .........
1768    To 13 Taxes @ 9/10/d/   6  7 10    V. .. By B WYNNS Jur. .... 6  7 10
  69    To 9 Do ... @ 10/6 ...  4 14  6    BW   By B: WYNNS Junr. .. 4 14  6
  70    To 9 Do ... @ 7/4 ....  3  6            Rec/d/. ............ 3  6 ..
                               1=4  8  4                            14  8  4
```

```
        James PHELPS .........
1768    To 1 Tax ............   -- 9 10
  69    To 2 Do . @ 10/6 .....  -1  1
  70    To 1 Do .............   ..  7  4
                                 1 18  2
```
==
```
(42) 42 James RIDDICK
1768    To 6 Taxes @ 9/10/d/ .  -2 19       V. .. By B. WYNNS Jur. ... 2 19 --
  69    To 5 Do .. @ 10/6 ....  2 12  6
  70    To =6 Do . @ 7/4 .....  2  4        By Procl. .............. 4 16  6
                                 7 15  6                             7 15  6
```

```
        Joseph NORFLEET
1768    To 1 Tax ............   -- 9 10     V. .. By B. WYNNS Jur. ...    9 10
  69    To 1 Do .............   -- 10  6
  70    To 1 Do .............   --  7  4    1770 By Procl ..........    .  7  4
                                 1  7  8                               (blank)
```

(42) (Cont.)
    John GREEN Jun/r/.

1768	To 1 Tax	--	9	10
69	To 1 Do	--	10	6
70	To 1 Do	..	7	4
		1	7	8

V. .. By B: WYNNS Jur 9 10

    Jesse OLEVENT.

1768	To 1 Tax	--	9	10
69	To 1 Do	--	10	6
		1	0	4

==

(43) 43 James ELLISS ....

1768	To 1 Tax	..	9	10
69	To 1 Do	..	10	6
70	To 2 Do . @ 7/4	..	14	8
		1	15	

V. .. By B. WYNNS Jur 9 10

    By Procl 14 8

    Jesse VANN ....

1768	To 3 Taxes @ 9/10/d/ .	1	9	6
69	To 3 Do .. @ 10/6	1	11	6
70	To 3 Do .. @ 7/4	1	2	
		4	3	

1768
1769 Rec/d/ 3 1
1770 Rec/d/ in part 14 8
Ballc? 7/4   3 15 8

    Jesse SANDERS

1768	To 4 Tax . @ 9/10/d/ .	1	19	4
69	To 4 Do .. @ 10/6	2	2	
70	To 3 Do .. @ 7/4	1	2	
		5	3	4

Rec/d/. 5 3 4

    Joshua LANG

1768	To 1 Tax	..	9	10
69	To 1 Do	--	10	6
70	To 1 Do	--	7	4
		1	7	8

==

(44) 44 Jesse JONES ....

| 1768 | To 1 Tax .... | .. | 9 | 10 |

    Jonathan FRYER.

1768	To 1 Tax	..	9	10
69	To 1 Do	..	10	6
		1	0	4

    Joseph ROOKS ....

1768	To 2 Taxes @ 9/10/d/ .	..	19	8
69	To 2 Do .. @ 10/6	1	1	
		2	0	8

V. .. By B. WYNNS Jur. ... 1 1 0

    John ELISS ....

1768	To 1 Tax	..	9	10
Sr. 69	To 1 Do	..	10	6
70	To 1 Do		7	4

==

(45) 45 Joseph RUNNELLS
1768   To 1 Tax 9 10

John CARTER
1768   To 3 Taxes @ 9/10/d/ . 1 9 6
 69   To 2 Do .. @ 10/6/d/ . 1 1   Rec/d/. 3 5
 70   To 2 Do .. @ 7/4 .... 14 8
                            3 5 2

James LANDING
1768   To 2 Taxes @ 9/10/d/ . -- 19 8
 69   To 1 Do .... --1̶7̶0̶ 6
 70   To 2 Do .. @ 7/4 ..... -- 14 8   By Procl .... 1 10 -
                            2 4 10

Isaac FRYER. ....
1768   To 1 Tax .... -- 9 10
 69   To 1 Do .... -- 10 6
 70   To 1 Do .... -- 7 4
                            1 7 8

James PARKER ....
1768   To 1 Tax .... -- 9 10
Sen/r/
 69   To 2 Do .. @ 10/6 .... 1 1
 70   To 2 Do .. @ 7/4 ..... -- 14 8
                            2 5 6

----

(46) 46 John ELLISS ....
1768   To 1 Tax .... -- 9 10
1770   To 1 Do .... -- 7 4
                            17 2

John HINES ....
1768   To 2 Taxes @ 9/10/d/ . .. 19 8

James EURE ....
1768   To 2 Taxes @ 9/10/d/ . .. 19 8   V. .. By B. WYNNS Jur 19 8
 69   To 3 Do .. @ 10/6 .... 1 11 6
Sen/r/ 70 To 2 Do .. @ 7/4 ... -- 14 8   Rec/d/. 2 6 2
                          3 5 10   3 5 10

Josiah LANGSTON ......
1768   To 1 Tax .... -- 9 10
 69   To 1 Do .... -- 10 6
                            1 0 4

==

(47) 47 Josiah PARKER
1768   To 1 Tax .... -- 9 10
 69   To 1 Do .... -- 10 6
 70   To 1 Do .... -- 7 4

Joseph SPEIGHT.

1768	To 11 Taxes @ 9/10/d/ .	5 8 2	V. .. By B. WYNNS Jur. ...	5 8 2
69	To 10 Do .. @ 10/6	5 5 -	... By Ben. WYNNS Junr.	0=535 =0
		10 13 2		10 13 =2

John ODAM ....

1768	To 6 Taxes @ 9/10/d/ .	2 19
69	To 6 Do .. @ 10/6	3 3 --
70	To 9 Do .. @ 7/4	3 6
		9 8

John DINNEY ....

1768	To 1 Tax	-- 9 10
69	To 1 Do	-- 10 6
		1 0 4

===

(48) 48 Jacob FRYER

1768	To 1 Tax	-- 9 10

James SMITH ....

1768	To 1 Tax	.. 9 10	V. .. By B. WYNNS Jur	9 10

Joseph WARREN ....

1768	To 1 Tax	. 9 10	V. .. By B. WYNNS Jur	9 10
69	To 1 Do	.. 10 6		
70	To 1 Do	.. 7 4	1770 Rec/d/	. 7 4
		1 7 8		

Jesse HARRELL ....

1768	To 1 Tax	.. 9 10	pd V.. By B. WYNNS Jur	9 10
69	To 1 Do	.. 10 6		
70	To 1 Do	.. 7 4	Rec/d/.	17 10
		1 07 8		1 7 8

James SAVAGE ....

1768	To 2 Taxes @ 9/10/d/ .	.. 19 8
69	To 2 Do .. @ 10/6	.1 1

===

(49) 49 John WALLISS ....

1768	To 2 Taxes @ 9/10	.. 19 8
69	To 1 Do	.. 10 6
		1 10 2

John SHEPHERD

1768	To 6 Taxes @ 9/10	2 19		
69	To 5 Do .. @ 10/6	.2 12 6	By Procl in part ...	2 14 8
70	To 7 Do .. @ 7/4	2 11 4		
		8 2 10		

Isaac PIPKIN ....Dr.

(49) (Cont.)
1768   To 8 Taxes @ 9/10/d/ . .3 18 10   V. .. By B. WYNNS Jur 3 18 10
  69   To 8 Do .. @ 10/6 .... .4 4 --
                                 8 2 10

        John ROSS ....
1768   To 1 Tax .... -- 9 10
  69   To 1 Do .... -- 10 6
  70   To 1 Do .... -- 7 4
                                1 7 8
==

(50) 50 James LANG ....
1768   To 1 Tax 9 10
  69   To 1 Do .... 10 6   BW   By B. WYNNS Jur 10 6
  70   To 2 Do .. @ 7/4 .... 14 8   1770 By Procl 14 8
                                 1 15 -

        James WELLS ....
1768   To 1 Tax .... -- 9 10
  69   To 1 Do .... -- 10 6
  70   To 1 Do .... -- 7 4
                                1. 7 8

        Joel GOODMAN ....
1768   To 5 Taxes @ 9/10/d/ . 2 9 2   V. .. By B. WYNNS Jur. 2 9 2
1770   To 5 Do .. @ 7/4 ..... 1 16 8   1770 By Procl 1 16 8
                                 4 5 10   4 5 10

        John PARKER Sen/r/. ....
1768   To 2 Taxes @ 9/10/d/ . .. 19 8
  69   To 3 Do .. @ 10/6 .... 1 11 6
  70   To 3 Do .. @ 7/4 ..... 1 2
                                 3 13 2
==

(51) 51 Josiah HARRELL ....
1768   To 1 Tax .... -- 9 10
  69   To 1 Do .... -- 10 6
  70   To 1 Do .... -- 7 4
                                1 7 8

        John HARRELL ....
1768   To 1 Tax 9 10

        John GATLING ....
1768   To 4 Taxes @ 9/10/d/ . .1 19 4   V. .. By B. WYNNS Jur 1 19 4
  69   To 4 Do .. @ 10/6 .... 2 2 ..   BW   By B. WYNNS Jur 2 2
                                 4 1 4
  70   To 4 Do .. @ 7/4 ..... 1 9 4   1770 By prol 1 9 4
                                 5 10 8   5 10 8

        John WATSON ....
1768   To 5 Taxes @ 9/10/d/ . .2 9 2
==

(52) 52 James OYZMOND ....
1768   To 1 Tax 9 10
  69   To 1 Do 10 6
                                  1 0 4

        Jane WILLIAMS ....
17689   To 2 Taxes @ 910/±06 .   1= 1= 0

        John WIGGINS ....
1768   To 1 Tax 9 10
  69   To 1 Do 10 6
  70   To 1 Do 7 4
                                  1 7 8

        Jethro HARRELL ....   By Procl 1 14 4
1769   To 2 Taxes @ 9/10 (sic) .. 19 8?
  70   To 2 Do .. @ 7/4 ..... -- 14 8
                                  1 14 4
===

(53) 53 Jacob WALTERS ....
1769   To 1 Tax .... 10 6   BW   By B: WYNNS Jur 10 6
  70   To 1 Do ....   -- 7 4   ... By prol 7 4
                                 17 10   17 10

        John HAMBLETON ....
1769   To 2 Taxes @ 10/6 .... .1 1
  70   To 1 Do 7 4
                                  1 8 4

        James RIDDICK Esqr. ..
1769   To 5 Taxes @ 10/6 .... 2 12 6   BW   By B: WYNNS Junr ... 2 12 6
  70   To 5 Do. . @ 7/4 ..... .1 16 8   By prol 1 16 8
                                  4 9 2   4 9 2

        James LUCAS ....
1769   To 1 Tax 10 6
===

(54) 54 James WALLACE ....
1769   To 2 Taxes @ 10/6 .... 1 11 --
  70   To 1 Do 7 4
                                  1 8 4   Rec/d/. 1 8 4

        John WEBB
1769   To 1 Tax 10 6

        John WOOD ....
1769   To 1 Tax 10 6
  70   To 1 Do ....   -- 7 4
                                 17 10

        Joseph GRIFFIN ....
1770   To 1 Tax 7 4

```
        Joseph PEELE
177=0   To 1 Tax ............  --  7  4
===========================================================================

(55) 55 Jeremiah CASE ........
1770    To 1 Tax .............  ..  7  4
---------------------------------------------------------------------------

        John LANG ...........
1770    To 1 Tax .............  ..  7  4
---------------------------------------------------------------------------

        John LEWIS
1770    To 10 Taxes ..........  3..13 4    1770  By Procl ............ .. 17 --
                                                 By Do .............. 2 16  4
---------------------------------------------------------------------------

        Joseph PLATT .........
1770    To 1 Tax .............  ..  7  4
---------------------------------------------------------------------------

        John MORRISS ........
1770    To 1 Tax .............  ..  7  4    1770- Rec/d/. ............. .  7  4
---------------------------------------------------------------------------

        James BOON Mixt. Blood
1770    To 1 Tax .............  ..  7  4
===========================================================================

(56) 56 Jesse HARRELL ........
1770    To 1 Tax .............  ..  7  4
---------------------------------------------------------------------------

        John BETHEYA ........
1770    To 2 Taxes @ 7/4/d/ ..  -- 14  8
---------------------------------------------------------------------------

        John MC. CONE ........
1768    To 1 Tax .............  --  9 10
  69    To 1 Do .............  -- 10  6
  70    To 1 Do .............  --  7  4
                                   1  7  8
---------------------------------------------------------------------------

        Jacob ODAM ...........
1768    To 1 Tax .............  ..  9 10
  69    To 1 Do .............  .. 10  6
                                   1  0  4
===========================================================================

(57) 57 Jacob WHEATLEY .......
1768    To 1 Tax .............  --  9 10
  69    To 21 Do @ 10/6 ......  .0 10  6   By Procl ..........  1  0  4
                                   1 00 04
---------------------------------------------------------------------------

        James PORTER .........
1768    To 5 Takes @ 9/10/d/ .  .2  9  2
  69    To 5 Do .. @ 10/6 ....  2 12  6    By abm?.. PORTER ...  8  7  8
  70    To 9 Do .. @ 7/4 .....  3  6
                                   8  7  8
---------------------------------------------------------------------------

        Isarael SCOTT ........
1768    To 1 Tax .............  ..  9 10   Rec/d/. ............   9 10
```

(57) (Cont.)
```
         John SANDEFER ........
1768     To 1 Tax .............   --  9 10        By prol ............  1 12 --
  69     To 2 Do @ 10/6 .......   .1  1 --
  70     To 1 Do .............    ..  7  4
                                  =1 1=8 2
```
===

```
(58) 58 James MANEY .........
1768     To 18 Taxes @ 9/10/d/   8  17  -        By Swap of Horses .. 12 10 --
  69     To 16 Do .. @ 10/6 ...  8   8   1785 (sic) By J. MANEY ........ 10 19  8
  70     To 17 Do .. @ 7/4 ....  6   4  8                                23  9  8
                                 23   9  8
```

```
         John MONTGOMERY ......
1768     To 5 Taxes @ 9/10 ....  2  9  2        By prol. ...........  2  6 -8-
  69     To 3 Do .. @ 10/6 ....  1 11  6
  70     To 4 Do .. @ 7/4 .....  1  9  4
                                 5 10
```

```
         John LEE ............
1768     To 1 Tax .............   ..  9 10      By order on the
  69     To 1 Do .............    .. 10  6      Church warden      1 16 --
  70     To 1 Do .............    ..  7  4
                                  1  7  8
```

```
       _ John REARDEN .........
1768     To 1 Tax .............   ..  9 10
  69     To 1 Do .............    .. 10  6
                                  1  0  4
```
===

```
(59) 59 Jesse BROWN ..........
1768     To 1 Tax .............   ..  9 10
  69     To 1 Do .............    .. 10  6
                                  1  0  4
```

```
         Jacob DICKERSON ......
1768     To 1 Tax .............   ..  9 10/d/
  69     To 1 Do .............    .. 10  6
  70     To 1 Do .............    ..  7  4
                                  1  7  8
```

```
         James FRYER .........
1768     To 2 Taxes @ 9/10/d/ .  .. 19  8      By C: EDWARDS ...... .. 18  5
  69     To 1 Do .............    .. 10  6
  70     To 1 Do .............    ..  7  4
              worrent (sic) 2/8   1 17  6
```

```
         John CROSS ........... Dr.
1768     To 1 Tax .............   ..  9 10
  69     To 1 Do .............    .. 10  6
                                  1  0  4
```
===

32

```
(60) 60 John SMITH ..........
1768    To 1 Tax ............. ..  9 10
  69    To 1 Do ............. .. 10  6        Rec/d/ ............. 1  7  8
  70    To 1 Do .............  ..  7  4
                                    1  7  8
--------------------------------------------------------------------------------
        James JONES .........
1768    To 1 Tax ............. ..  9 10
--------------------------------------------------------------------------------
        James Van Vin VIRDE ..
1768    To 1 Tax ............. ..  9 10
--------------------------------------------------------------------------------
1768 (sic) John SCOTT .......
        To 1 Tax .............  --  9 10
~~1770~~ To 2 Do @ 7/4 ........  -- 14  8        By Procl. .......... 1  4  6
                                    1  4  6
--------------------------------------------------------------------------------
        John BOYCE ..........
1768    To 1 Tax .............  --  9 10
================================================================================
(61) 61 John HUBBARD ........
1768    To 1 Tax .............  --  9 10
  69    To 1 Do ............. .. 10  6
  70    To 1 Do ............. ..  7  4
                                    1  7  8
--------------------------------------------------------------------------------
        Jonas BIRD ..........
1768    To 1 Tax ............. ..  9 10
  69    To 1 Do ............. .. 10  6
  70    To 1 Do ............. ..  7  4        By Procl .......... 1  /?--
                                    1  7  8
--------------------------------------------------------------------------------
        John MOTT ...........
1768    To 1 Tax .............  --  9 10
  69    To 1 Do .............  -- 10  6
--------------------------------------------------------------------------------
        Isaac CARTER Sen/r/ ..          1773
1768    To 14 Taxes @ 9/10 ...  6 17  8   march 4  Rec/d/. ......... 9  4 5 1/2
  69    To 14 Do .. @ 10/6 ...  7  7              Rec/d/. ......... 10 17 6 1/2
  70    To 16 Do .. @ 7/4 ....  5 17  4                             20  2 --
                               20 10? 02
================================================================================
(62) 62 John MOORE Sen/r/.              By Procl .......... 4
1768    To 8 Taxes @ 9/10 ....  3 18 10    By Ballce. acct. ... 1  0  3 1/2
  69    To 8 Do .. @ 10/6 ....  4  4                            5  0  3 1/2
  70    To 9 Do .. @ 7/4 .....  3  6    1778  By prol ............ 1 10 -----
                               11  8 10  Feb. 24  By 8 Dolers (sic) . 3  4 -----
To Thos. DAVIS .............. 2 .. ..                            9 14  3 1/2
                               13 -8 10         By paid in full .... 3 14  6
                               ==== 8+8+8?1/2=======Cost 13  8  9 1/2
--------------------------------------------------------------------------------
        Josiah SUMNER.
1768    To 5 Taxes @ 9/10/d/ .  2  9  2        Rec/d/ ............. 9  1  4
  69    To 7 Do .. @ 10/6 ....  3 13  6
```

(62) (Cont.)
```
  70     To 8 Do .. @ 7/4 .....    2 18  8
                                    9  1  4
```

```
         Jesse WESTON ........
1768     To 3 Taxes @ 9/10/d/ .  1  9  6         By prol ............  3 12 6
Pat/r/ 69 To 2 Do . @ 10/6 ...   1  1
  70     To 3 Do .. @ 7/4 .....   1  2
                                  3 12  6
```

```
         John PINNER ..........
1768     To 1 Tax .............  --  9 10        By Procl ...........  1  3  4
  69     To 1 Do ..............  -- 10  6
  70     To 1 Do ..............  --  7  4
                                  1  7  8
         To Cost of Warrt .....      2  8
```

==

```
(63) 63 James RASBERRY
1768     To 2 Taxes @ 9/10/d/ .  -- 19  8        By B: WYNNS ........  2  8
  69     To 2 Do ..............   1  1           By Cost of worant ..  .  2  8
  70     To 1 Do ..............  --  7  4                              2 10  8
                                  2  8
         To Cost of worrant ...     2  8
                                  2 10  8
```

```
         John WILLOUGHBY ......
1768     To 1 Tax .............  --  9 10
  69     To 1 Do ..............  -- 10  6
  70     To 1 Do ..............  ..  7  4        By Jesse BIRD ......  1  7  8
                                  1  7  8
```

```
         Jeremiah MICHENER
1768     To 1 Tax .............  ..  9 10
```

```
         James HEDGSPETH ......
1768     To 1 Tax .............  --  9 10        Rec/d/ .............  1  7  8
  69     To 1 Do ..............  -- 10  6
  70     To 1 Do ..............  --  7  4
                                  1  7  8
```

==

```
(64) 64 James HARRISS ........
1768     To 3 Taxes @ 9/10/d/ .  1  9  6         Rec/d/ .............  3  ...
  69     To 3 Do .. @ 10/6 ....  1 11  6
  70     To 6 Do ...@ 7/4 .....  2  4
                                 5  5
```

```
         James SPARKMAN
1768     To 1 Tax .............  --  9 10
  69     To 1 Do ..............  -- 10  6
  70     To 1 Do ..............  --  7  4
                                  1  7  8
```

----

(64) (Cont.)
　　　John CLARKE Jun/r/ .....
1768　To 1 Tax ....　-- 9 10
　69　To 1 Do ....　-- 10　6
　70　To 1 Do ....　-- 7　4
　　　　　　　　　　　　　　1　7　8

　　　Jacob FREEMAN
1768　To 2 Taxes @ 9/10 ....　.. 19 6?8?　　By Procl ....　1 14 10
　69　To 1 Do ....　.. 10　6　　　　By P Do ....　. 10 ..
　70　To 2Do ... @ 7/4 .....　.. 1=4=8?　　　　　　　　　　　　　2　4 10
　　　　　　　　　　　　　　2　4　10

===

(65) 65 John ALPHIN ....
1768　To 1 Tax ....　-- 9 10
　69　To 1 Do ....　-- 10　6
　　　　　　　　　　　　　　1　0　4

　　　James MC. GLOHON
1768　To 4 Taxes @ 9/10/d/ .　1 19　4
　69　To 4 Do .. @ 10/6 ....　2　2　-
　70　To 2 Do .. @ 7/4 .....　-- 14　8
　　　　　　　　　　　　　　4 16

　　　John NORTHCOTT ....
1768　To 4 Taxes @ 9/10 ....　1 19　4
　69　To 1 Do ....　. 10　6
　70　To 1 Do ....　-- 7　4
　　　　　　　　　　　　　　2 17　2

　　　Josiah ASKEW ....
1768　To 2 Taxes @ 9/10/d/ .　-- 19　8
　69　To 2Do ... @ 10/6 ....　1　1　-
　　　　　　　　　　　　　　2 .. 8

===

(66) 66 John LIVERMON ....
1768　To 1 Tax ....　-- 9 10
　69　To 1 Do ....　-- 10　6
　70　To 1 Do ....　-- 7　4
　　　　　　　　　　　　　　1　7　8

　　　James NICKENS ....
1768　To 2 Taxes @ 9/10/d/ .　.. 19　8　　Rec/d/ ....　3　5 10
　69　To 3 Do .. @ 10/6 ....　1 11　6
　70　To 2 Do .. @ 7/4 .....　-- 14　8
　　　　　　　　　　　　　　3　5 10

　　　James OVERNTON ....
1768　To 1 Tax ....　-- 9 10
1770　To 2 Do @ 7/4 ....　-- 14　8
　　　　　　　　　　　　　　1　4　6　　Rec/d/ ....　1　4　6

35

(66) (Cont.)
```
        Joseph PENDER ........
1768    To 1 Tax .............  -- 9 10          By Procl ........... 1  7  8
  69    To 1 Do .............  -- 10  6
  70    To 1 Do .............  --  7  4
                                 1  7  8
```

===

(67) 67 John REID (Clk)
```
1768    To 4 Taxes @ 9/10 ....  1 19  4
```

```
        John COPELAND ........
1768    To 5 Taxes @ 9/10/d/ .  2  9  2
  69    To 3 Do .. @ 10/6 ....  1 11  6
(blank) To 3 Do .. @ 7/4 .....  -1  2  -          By Procl. .......... 5  2  8
                                 5  2  8
```

```
        Jacob SMITH ..........
1768    To 2 Taxes @ 9/10 ....  -- 19  8          By B. WYNNS Jur .... 2 11 12
  69    To 3 Do .. @ 10/6 ....  1 11  6
                                 2 11  2
```

```
        James COPELAND
1768    To 3 Taxes @ 9/10 ....  1  9  6           By Procl ........... 3 15
  69    To 3 Do .. @ 10/6 ....  1 11  6
  70    To 2 Do .. @ 7/4 .....  -- 14  8
                                 3 15
```
===

(68) 68 Joshua BAKER ....
```
1768    To 1 Tax .............  -- 9 10
  69    To 1 Do .............  -- 10  6
  70    To 1 Do .............  --  7  4
                                 1  7  8
```

```
        John HARE /D. C
1768    To 9 Taxes @ 9/10/d/ .  4  8  6           Recd ==========
  70    To 8 Do .. @ 7/4 .....  2 18  8           Rec/d/ ............. 4  8  6
                                 7  7  2           Rec/d/ ............. 2 18  8
                                                                        7  7  2
```

```
        John BAKER Esqr ......           1775
1768    To 23 Taxes @ 9/10/d/  11  6  2  May 23 By Procl in full    32..5..10
  69    To 22 Do ======= @ 10/6 11 11
        To 1 Chair with 2 Wheels 1
  70    To 23 Do @ 7/4 .......  -8  8  8
                                32  5 10
```

```
        John Augs. WYNNS .....
1768    To 4 Taxes @ 9/10/d/ .  1 19  4          Rec/d/. .................. 4 16
  69    To 4 Do .. @ 10/6 ....  2  2  -
  70    To 2 Do .. @ 7/4 .....  -- 14  8
                                 4 16 --
```
===

```
(69) 69 Jonas TAYLOR .........
1768    To 2 Taxes @ 9/10/d/ .  -- 19  8
  69    To 2 Do .. @ 10/6 ....   1  1
  70    To 2 Do .. @ 7/4 .....  -- 14  8
                                 2 15  4   68:69:& 70 By Colo.. WYNNS Promise 2 15 4
```

```
        Isaac LEWIS ..........
1768    To 1 Tax .............  --  9 10
  69    To 2 Do .. @ 10/6 ....   1  1           By Procl ........... 2  5  6
  70    To 2 Do .. @ 7/4 .....  -- 14  8
                                 2  5  6
```

```
        James BOON Esqr ......
1768    To 4 Taxes @ 9/10/d/ .   1 19  4        Rec/d/. ............. 1 19  4
```

```
        John SPEIGHT .........
1768    To __ Taxes @ 9/10/d/    4 18  4        By prol ............ 13 13  6
  69    To 9 Do Search @ 10/6    4 14  6
  70    To 11 Do .. @ 7/4 ....   4  0  8
                                13 13  6
```

```
(70) 70 Jonas LASSITER
1768    To 1 Tax .............  --  9 10
  69    To 1 Do .............   -- 10  6
  70    To 1 Do. Stalins (sic)  --  7  4
                                 1  7  8
```

```
        James BURRUSS ........
1768    To 2 Taxes @ 9/10/d/ .  -- 19  8
  69    To 1 Do .............   -- 10  6
                                 1 10  2
```

```
        Joshua BURRUSS .......
1768    To 1 Tax .............  --  9 10        By Procl ...........    9 10
```

```
        James BAKER Con/st/. ...
1768    To 1 Tax .............  --  9 10
  69    To 3 Do. @ 10/6 ......   1 11  6
  70    To 3 Do @ 7/4 .......    1  2---        paid .............. 3  3  4
                                 3  3  4
```

```
(71) 71 James NOWELL .........
17768   To 1 Tax .............  ..  9 10
  69    To 1 Do .............   .. 10  6
  70    To 1 Do .............   ..  7  4
                                 1  7  8
```

```
        James BYRUM ..........
1768    To 1 Tax .............  --  9 10
  69    To 1 Do .............   -- 10  6
  70    To 1 Do .............   --  7  4
                                 1  7  8
```

(71) (Cont.)

	John BAKER /Killum ...					By Robt. FAIRLESS ..	2	5	6
1768	To 4 Taxes @ 9/10/d/ .	1	19	4		By Ditto	1	10	--
69	To 4 Do .. @ 10/6	2	2	-		By prol	2	3	6
70	To 6 Do .. @ 7/4	.2	4			By Do		6	4
		6	5	4			6	5	4

	John MAYNOR				1768	By Procl	9 10/d/
17768	To 1 Tax	--	9 10			By H MURFREE had of }	1 5 8
69	To 2 Do @ 10/6	-1	1			Wm. JENKINS for you}	1 15 68
70	To 2 Do @ 7/4	-- 14	8			Balls. 10/ Judgt. Recd.	10--
		2	5	6			2 5 6

===

(72) 72 Joseph WATSFORD

1768	To 1 Tax	--	9 10
69	To 2 Do @ 10/6	-1	1
		1	10 10

	Joseph GREEN				By Procl	1	-	-
1768	To 1 Tax	--	9 10		By Procl		12	
69	To 2 Do @ 10/6	.1	1 --					
70	To 1 Do	-- 7	4					
		1 18	2					

	Isaac HILL			
1768	To 4 Taxes @ 9/10/d/ .	1	19	4
69	To 3 Do .. @ 10/6	1 11	6	
		3 10	10	

By Procl 3 10 10

	James JONES			
1768	To 7 Taxes @ 9/10/d/ .	3	8	10
69	To 9 Do .. @ 10/6	4	14	6
70	To 8 Do .. @ 7/4	2	18	8
		19?62		

===

(73) 73 Jesse QUINBY ....

1768	To 1 Tax	--	9 10
6970	To 1 Do	-- 7	4
		17	2

By Procl 17 2

	John REIDE			
1768	To 3 Taxes @ 9/10/d/ .	1	9	6
69	To 5 Do .. @ 10/6	2	12	6
70	To 5 Do .. @ 7/4	1 16	8	
		5 18	8	

	Joseph WYYNS			
1768	To 4 Taxes @ 9/10/d/ .	1	19	4
69	To 4 Do .. @ 10/6	2	2	
70	To 2 Do .. @ 7/4	. 14	8	
		4 16		

----

(73) (Cont.)
```
        James DAWS ...........
1768    To 2 Taxes @ 9/10/d/ .   -- 19  8
  69    To 2 Do .. @ 10/6 ....    1  1          if not paid by J SPIGHT
  70    To 1 Do ..............    --  7  4
                                   2  8
```
===

(74) 74 John SUMMERS
```
1768    To 1 Tax .............  ..  9 10
```

```
        John FLEMMON .........
1768    To 1 Tax .............  ..  9 10
```

```
        Isaac PERRY ..........
1768    To 1 Tax .............  ..  9 10
  69    To 1 Do ..............  .. 10  6
  70    To 1 Do ..............  ..  7  4        By Procl ..........  1  7  8
                                  1  7  8
```

```
        Joseph HOBBS .........
1769    To 2 Taxes @ 10/6 ....    1  1          By 2 Dolers ........  . 16  -
  70    To 2 Do .. @ 7/4 .....   -- 14  8        By prol. ...........      5
        Cost. worant (sic)        1 15  8
```

```
        Joseph DARDEN Cons/t/.
1769    To 1 Tax .............  .. 10  6        By prol. ...........  . 10  6
```
===

(75) 75 John BOON ....
```
1769    To 1 Tax .............  . 10  6
  70    To 2 Do @ 7/4 ........  .. 14  8        By Procl ..........  1  5  2
                                  1  5  2
```

```
        James WHEATLEY .......
1769    To 2 Taxes @ θ 10/6 ..    1  1
  70    To 2 Do .. @ 7/4/d/ ..  . 14  8         Rec/d/ .............. 1 15  8
                                  1 15  8
```

```
        Isaac HALL ...........
1769    To 1 Tax .............  -- 10  6
```

```
        Jonathan RAGERS ......
1769    To 2 Taxes @ 10/6 ....    1  1          By paid in the old list    2  3
  70    To 3 Do .. @ 7/4 .....    1  2
                                  2  3
```
===

(76) 76 John ALEXANDER ....
```
1769    To 4 Taxes @ 10/6 ....    2  2          By Procl ..........  5  8  4
        To 1 Chair with 2 wheels  1              By Procl ..........  .. 3
  70    To 4 Taxes @ 7/4/d/ ..    1  9  4                              5..11..4
        To 1 Chair with 2 wheels  1
                                  5 11  4
```

39

(76) (Cont.)

Joseph MOORE ....
17689   To 2 Taxes @ 10/6 ....   1 1   1769 By Proclama?. 1 1

Jesse COPELAND ....
1769   To 2 Taxes @ 10/6 ....   1 1   By Procl 1 10
  70   To 3 Do .. @ 7/4 .....   1 2   By Procla?   13
                                  2 3   2 3

John CARRILL ....
1769   To 6 Taxes @ 10/6 ....   3 3   Rec/d/. by Mrs. HILL 3 3

Joshua RAWLES ....
1769   To 1 Tax 10 6

==

(77) 77 John BIRD ....
1769   To 1 Tax 10 6
  70   To 1 Do .... -- 7 4
                                 17 10

Joseph DANIEL ....
1769   To 1 Tax 10 6
  70   To 3 Do @ 7/4 ....   1 2   Rec/d/. 1 12 6
                                  1 12 6

James HOWARD. Sen/r/.
1769   To 3 Taxes @ 170/46...   1 1=1?6   By Procl 1 16 2
  70   To 2 Do .. @ 7/4 .... 14 8   By prol. 10 0
                                  2 6 2   2 6 2

James HAILE ....
1769   To 1 Tax .... -- 10 6   1769 By Procl. 10 6
  70   To 2 Do @ 7/4 .... -- 14 8   12 -
                                  1 5 2

James CARTER ....
                                                     By prol 17 6
1769   To 2 Taxes @ 10/6 ....   1 1   By procl 3 6
                                                                          £ 1: 1 -

==

(78) 78 Jesse HAILE ....
1769   To 1 Tax 10 6
  70   To 1 Do .... -- 7 4   By prol. 17 10
                                   17 10

John BEAMAN ....
1769   To 1 Tax .... 190±06
  70   To 1 Do 7 4
                                   17 10

James WRIGHT ....
1769   To 10 Taxes @ 7/10/6 .   5 5 -
  70   To 10 Do .. @ 7/4 ....   3 13 4   Rec/d/ 8 18 04
                                  8 18 4

40

(78) (Cont.)
      John HOGGARD
1769   To 1 Tax 10 6

        John Nicholas SMITH
1769   To 1 Tax 10 6
==

(79) 79 Joseph DICKINSON
1769   To 5 Taxes @ 10/6 .... 2 12 6   By prol. 2 12 6

        John VAN PELT
1769   To 5 Taxes @ 10/6 .... 2 12 6

        Jethro DOUGHTIE
1769   To 1 Tax ....   10 6   By Procl 10 6

        Isaac SAUNDERS
1769   To 1 Tax .... 10 6   Rec/d/. 10 6

        James BELCH ....
1769   To 1 Tax .... 10 6   By Procl 10 6
==

(80) 80 James STEWARD ....
1769   To 1 Tax 10 6

        Jesse WALTERS ....
1769   To 1 Tax 10 6

        John WILLIAMS ....
1769   To 1 Tax .... - 10 6   By W M Rec/d/. 17 10
  70   To 1 Do .... -- 7 4
                                  17 10

        James OUTLAW ....
1769   To 1 Tax 10 6
  70   To 1 Do 7 4
                                  17 10

        Jacob HAYSE ....
1769   To 2 Taxes @ 10/6 ....   1 1
==

(81) 81 Isaac WILLIAMS ....
1770   To 2 Taxes @ 7/4 .... 14 8   Rec/d/. 14 8

        -Josiah MELTIAH ....
1770   To 2 Taxes @ 7/4 .... 14 8   By Procl 7 4

        James GAY ....
1770   To 1 Tax .... 7 4   1770 By Procl 7 4

        John BREWER ....
1770   To 4 Taxes @ 7/4 .....   1 9 4

(81) (Cont.)
```
        John WILLIAMS ........
1770    To 3 Taxes @ 7/4 .....   1  2  -
```
===

```
(82) 82 John DARDEN .........
1770    To 3 Taxes @ 7/4 .....   1  2
```

```
        James BRITT .........
1770    To 1 Tax .............  --  7  4
```

```
        James WILKINS ........
1770    To 1 Tax .............  --  7  4          By Procl ........... ..  7  4
```

```
        Jethro DARDEN ........
1770    To 12 Taxes @ 7/4 ....      4  8
```

```
        John OZELL ..........
1770    To 1 Tax ............. ..  7  4
```

```
        James COOK ..........
1770    To 1 Tax ............. ..  7  4
```
===

```
(83) 83 John COALSTON Sen/r/.
1770    To 1 Tax ............. ..  7  4
```

```
        John GILBERT. ........
1770    To 2 Taxes @ 7/4 ..... -- 14  8          By Procl. ........... .. 14  8
```

```
        John BISHOP .........
1770    To 2 Taxes @ 7/4 ..... -- 14  8          By Procl. ........... .. 14  8
```

```
        James DENTON ........
1770    To 2 Taxes @ 7/4 ..... -- 14  8          Rec/d/. ............. .. 14  8
```

```
        James MURFREE ........
1770    To 4 Taxes @ 7/4 .....   1  9  4         Rec/d/. of the Extx  1  9  4
```
===

```
(84) 84 Jacob ARCHER .........
1770    To 2 Taxes @ 7/4 ....: -- 14  8
```

```
        Jesse FLOOD .........
1770    To 1 Tax .............  --  7  4
```

```
        Jesse WILLIAMS .......
1770    To 3 Taxes @ 7/4 .....   1  2  -    1770 By Procl. .......... . 10  8
                                                 By Do ..............  . 11  4
                                                                        1  2  -
```

```
        Jonathan ROBERTS Esqr.
1770    To 5 Taxes @ 7/4 .....   1 16  8         By Procl. .......... 1..16..8
```
----

(84) (Cont.)
```
          John MERITT .........
1770      To 1 Tax .............  --  7  4
```

```
          Joseph JONES .........
1770      To 7 Taxes @ 7/4 .....  2 11  4      1770  By Procl. ...........2 11  4
```
==

(85) 85 James WALKER ....
```
1770      To 1 Tax .............  --  7  4
```

```
          John BROWN Jun/r/.
1770      To 4 Taxes @ 7/4/d/ ..  1  9  4             Rec/d/. ............  1  9  4
```

```
          Josiah BURKETT .......
1770      To 2 Taxes @ 7/4/d/ .. -- 14  8
```

```
          John STEVENS .........
1770      To 4 Taxes @ 7/4/d/ ..  1  9  4      1770  By James COLEMAN    1  9  4
```

```
          Jane BROWN ..........
1770      To 1 Tax .............  --  7  4
```
==

(86) 86 Josiah BROWN ....
```
1770      To 2 Taxes @ 7/4 .....  .. 14  8      1770  By Procl. ..........  . 14  8/d/
1769      To 3 Do .. @ 10/6 ....  .1 11  6      1769  By Procl. ..........  1  5  4
                                  ------               By prol ............     6  2
                                  2  6  2                                   ------
                                                                           2  6  2
```

```
          John HARE/PT .........
1770      To 10 Taxes @ 7/4 ....  .3 13  4             By prol. ...........  3 13  4
```

```
          Ismy RASCO ..........
1770      To 4 Taxes @ 7/4 .....  1  9  4             Rec/d/. ............  1  9  4
```

```
          Jethro WILLIAMS ......
1770      To 2 Taxes @ 7/4 ..... -- 14  8      1770  By Procl. ..........  . 14  8
```

```
          Jesse RALLS .........
1770      To 1 Tax .............  --  7  4
```
==

(87) 87 John CARTER ....
```
1770      To 5 Taxes @ 7/4 .....  1 16  8             By 4 Dolers ........  1 12
```

```
          Colo. John BROWN .....
1770      To 10 Taxes @ 7/4/d/ .  3 13  4
```

```
          John SCEARS .........
1770      To 1 Tax .............  --  7  4             Rec/d. ............     7  4
```

```
          Jonathan CULLINS
1770      To _ Tax .............  --  7  4
```
----

(87) (Cont.)
```
        Jacob ARCHER .........
1770    To 2 Taxes @ 7/4 .....  -- 14  8
```
==

(88) 88 James ASKEW ....
```
1770    To 1 Tax .............  .  7  4          Rec/d/. ............   7  4
```

```
        Jernett COTTON .......
1770    To 1 Tax .............  ..  7  4
```

```
        James HEDGSPETH ......
1770    To 1 Tax .............  ..  7  4
68      To 1 Ditto ...........  ..  9 10
69      To 1 Ditto ...........  .. 10  6
                                  1  7  8?
```

```
        Jacob KEEL ...........
1770    To 4 Taxes @ 7/4 .....  -1  9  4        By Procl. .......... 1  9  4
```

```
        John VARLIN ..........
1770    To 1 Tax .............  -  7  4
```
==

(89) 89 James HOOKER
```
1770    To 5 Taxes @ 7/4 .....  1 16  8        By Procl. .......... 1 16  8
```

```
        Jonas QUINBY .........
1770    To 1 Tax .............  --  7  4
```

```
        John WILLIAMS Jun/r/.
1770    To 1 Tax .............  --  7  4     1770  By Procl. .......... .  7  4
```

```
        Jacob PARKER .........
1770    To 1 Tax .............  --  7  4
```

```
        Jesse RUNNELLS .......
1770    To 2 Taxes @ 7/4 .....  -- 14  8
```
==

(90) 90 John WILLIAMS Sen/r/.
```
1770    To 1 Tax .............  --  7  4
```

```
        James COTTON .........
1770    To 2 Taxes @ 74 ......  -- 14  8        By prol .............. 14  8
```

```
        Keziah DOUGLIS .......
1768    To 1 Tax .............  --  9 10
```

```
        Kirney GODWIN ........
1769    To 2 Taxes @ 10/6 ....  .1  1
70      To 2 Do .. @ 7/4 .....  -- 14  8        By Jesse BIRD ...... 1 15  8
                                 1 15  8
```
----

(90) (Cont.)
Luke PARKER ....
```
1768    To 1 Tax .............  --  9 10
  69    To 1 Do .............  -- 10  6
  70    To 1 Do .............  --  7  4      BW    By B. WYNNS Jur ....   7  4
                               ---------
                                1  7  8
```
==

(91) 91 Lamuel RABY ....
```
1769    To 1 Tax .............  -- 10  6
```

Capt. Lawrence BAKER
```
1769    To 7 Taxes @ 10/6 ....  3 13  6      1769   By Procl ...........  3 13  6
  70    To 10 Do . @ 7/4 .....  3 13  4             By Procl ...........  3 13  4
                               ---------                                 ---------
                                7  6 10                                   7  6 10
```

Lewis BRADDY ....
```
1770    To 1 Tax .............  --  7  4             By Procl ........... ..  7  4
```

Levey LEE ....
```
1770    To 2 Tax @ 7/4 .......  -- 14  8             By Procl ........... . 14  8
```

Lish DARDEN ....
```
1768    To 1 Tax .............  --  9 10
```
==

(92) 92 Littleton MANLEY .....
```
1768    To 2 Tax . @ 9/10 ....  -- 19  8
1769    To 3 Do .. @ 10/6 ....  .1 11  6             By prol. ...........  3  5 10
  70    To 2 Do .. @ 7/4 .....  -- 14  8
                               ---------
                                3  5 10
```

Lewis WILLIAMS ....
```
1768    To 3 Taxes @ 9/10 ....   1  9  6
  69    To 3 Do .. @ 10/6 ....  .1 11  6
  70    To 2 Do .. @ 7/4 .....  -- 14  8
                               ---------
                                3 15  8
```

Luke LANGSTON ....
```
1770    To 5 Taxes @ 7/4 .....   1 16  8             Rec/d/. ............  1 16  8
```

Luke HARE ....
```
1770    To 3 Taxes @ 7/4 .....   1  2               By Procl ...........  1  2
```
==

(93) 93 Lewis POWELL
```
1770    To 2 Taxes @ 7/4 .....  -- 14  8
```

Micajah RIDDICK ......
```
1768    To 2 Taxes @ 9/10/d/ .  -- 19  8      V. .. By B: WYNNS Jur ..... .. 19  8
  70    To 2 Do .. @ 7/4 .....  -- 14  8      1770  By prol.. ...........  . 14  8
                               ---------                                 ---------
                                1 14  4                                   1 104  4
```
----

(93) (Cont.)
        Mosses PARKER Jun/r/
1768   To 1 Tax .... -- 9 10
  69   To 1 Do .... -- 10 6
                               1 0 4

        Mary FELTON ....
1768   To 1 Tax .... -- 9 10
  69   To 1 Do .... -- 10 6
  70   To 2 Do ..@ 7/4 ...... -- 14 8   By Procl .... -- 14 8
                               1 15 -

==

(94) 94 Mosses SPIVEY ....
1768   To 2 Taxes @ 9/10/d/ . -- 19 8   By Procl 19 8
  69   To 3 Do .. @ 10/6 .... .1 11 6   By Procl 2 13 6
  70   To 3 Do .. @ 7/4 ..... 1 2 -   2 13? 6
                               3 13 2   3 13 2

        Mosse (sic) BOYCE Jun/r/
1768   To 2 Taxes @ 9/10/d/ . -- 19 8   V. .. By B: WYNNS Jur 19 8
  69   To 1 Do .... -- 10 6
  70   To 1 Do .... -- 7 4   Recd 7 4
                               (blank)

        Mosses HYNES ....
1768   To 1 Tax .... - 9 10   V. .. By B. WYNNS Jur. 9 10
  69   To 1 Do .... - 10 6   By Colo. SUMNER   - 17 10
  70   To 1 Do .... -- 7 4   1 7 8
                               1 7 8

     _ Mosses BOYCE ....
1768   To 1 Tax .... -- 9 10
  69   To 3 Do @ 10/6 .... 1 11 6
  70   To 3 Do @ 7/4 .... 1 2   By Colo. SUMNER   3 3 4
                               3 4 4 (sic)

==

(95) 95 Mosses HARE ....
1768   To 11 Taxes @ 9/10 ... 5 8 2   BW   By B: WYNNS 5 8 2

        Matthias GREEN
1768   To 1 Tax .... - 9 10
  69   To 1 Do .... -- 10 6
                               1 0 4

        Mosses LANGSTON ......
1768   To 1 Tax .... -- 9 10
  70   To 1 Do .... -- 7 4
                               16 8?

        Michael TAYLOR ....
1768   To 1 Tax .... -- 9 10

==

```
(96) 96 Mosses PARKER Sen/r/.
1769    To 1 Tax .............  -- 10  6
 70     To 1 Do .............   -- 7  4
                                  17 10
---------------------------------------------------------------------

        Mary VANN ...........
1769    To 1 Tax .............  -- 10  6
 70     To 1 Do .............   -- 7  4
                                  17 10
---------------------------------------------------------------------

        Martha HARE .........
1769    To 1 Tax .............  -- 10  6
---------------------------------------------------------------------

        Mary HARE ...........
1769    To 8 Taxes @ 10/6 ....  4  4      V. .. By BenjnWYNNS Jur.   4  4  -
=====================================================================

(97) 97 Mosses KITTRELL ......
1770    To 2 Taxes @ 7/4 .....  -- 14  8
---------------------------------------------------------------------

        Michael RUNNELLS
1768    To 1 Tax .............  --  9 10     Rec/d/ .............  1  7  8
 69     To 1 Do .............   -- 10  6
 70     To 1 Do .............   --  7  4
                                 1  7  8
---------------------------------------------------------------------

        Martha HOLLAMON
1768    To 4 Taxes @ 9/10/d/ .  1 19  4      Rec/d/. ............  3  6  -
1769    To 3 Do .. @ 10/6 .... .1 11  6      By Procl ..........  1 14  2
 70     To 4 Do .. @ 7/4 .....  1  9  4                           5  0  2
                                 5  0  2
---------------------------------------------------------------------

        Capt. Mosses SUMNER
1768    To 12 Taxes @ 9/10/d/ . 5 18  -      Rec/d/. in part .... 7  9  8
 69     To 13 Do .. @ 10/6 .... 6 16  6      Rec/d/ ............. 10  -  2
 70     To 13 Do .. @ 7/4 ..... 4 15  4                           17  9 10
                                 17  9 10
=====================================================================

(98) 98 Matthias BRICKELL Esq/r/.
17768   To 11 Taxes @ 9/10 ...  5  8  2      By prol. ........... 16  8  6
        To 1 Chair with 2 wheels 1
 69     To 10 Taxes @ 710/6 ..  5  5  -
        To 1 Chair with 2 wheels 1
 70     To 10 Taxes @ 7/4 .... -3 13  4
                                 16 68  6
---------------------------------------------------------------------

        Mosses MANLEY ........
1768    To 2 Taxes @ 9/10/d/ .  - 19  8     W. Rcd By B: WYNNS Jur. ..  19  8
---------------------------------------------------------------------

        Michael HILL .........
1768    To 1 Tax .............  --  9 10
 69     To 1 Do .............   -- 10  6     By Procl ..........  1  .  4
                                 1  0  4
---------------------------------------------------------------------
```

(98) (Cont.)
      Malichi GREEN ....
1768   To 1 Tax ....   - 9 10

==

(99) 99 Mosses MOORE ....
1769   To 1 Tax .... -- 10 6
 70   To 1 Do ....   -- 7 4   By Shadrick MOORE   7 10
                              17 10

      Mason BISHOP over Seer for C POLLOCK
1769   To 7 Taxes @ 10/6 .... 3 13 6
 70   To 8 Do .. @ 7/4 ..... 2 18 8
                       6 12 2

      Michael WARD ....
1769   To 5 Taxes @ 10/6 .... 2 12 6
 70   To 5 Do .. @ 7/4 ..... 1 16 8   Rec/d/. 4 9 2
                       4 9 2

      Nicholas KING ....
1768   To 3 Taxes @ 9/10/d/ . 1 9 6   V.
 69   To 3 Do .. @ 10/6 .... 1 11 6   V. .. By B. WYNNS Jur 3 1
 70   To 4 Do .. @ 7/4 ..... 1 9 4   1770 By Procl 1 9 4
                       4 10 4   4 10 4

==

(100) 100 Nathaniel HARGROVES
1768   To 1 Tax 9 10
 69   To 3 Do @ 10/6 .... 1 11 6
                       2 1 4

      Nehemiah KING ....
1770   To =1 Taxes @ 7/4 .... .. 7 4

      Nathan WHEATLEY ......
1768   To 1 Tax 9 10

      Nathan BRITT ....
1768   To 1 Tax 9 10

      Nanny FLOOD ....   By prol 5 2
1768   To 1 Tax .... 9 10   By prol. 4 8
                                                9 10

==

(101) 101 Nehemiah KNIGHT ....
1768   To 1 Tax .... 9 10   Rec/d/. 9 10

      Nathan MORRISS ....
1768   To 1 Tax 9 10

      Nehemiah REIGN ....
1768   To 10 Taxes @ 9/10/d/ .4 18 8

----

(101) (Cont.)
```
        Peter PARKER .........
1768    To 3 Taxes @ 9/10/d/ .   1  9  6        V. .. By B. WYNNS Jur. ...  1  9  6
  69    To 3 Do @ 10/6 .......   1 11  6
  70    To 3 Do @ 7/4 ........   1  2  -
                                 ---------
                                 4 23  -
```

```
        Ozias BEAMON .........
1770    To 3 Taxes @ 7/4 .....   1  2            By Procl ........... 1  2
```
==

(102) 102 Obediah SOWELL ......
```
1770    To 3 Taxes @ 7/4         1  2
```

```
        Peter HARRELL ........
1768    To 1 Tax .............   .  9 10        V. .. By B. WYNNS Jur ....  . 9 10
```

```
        Patience WARRIN ......
1770    To 1 Tax .............   .. .7  4
```

```
        Phillip WINBORN ......
1770    To 1 Tax .............   .  7  4
```

```
        Phillip RAILEY .......
1768    To 1 Tax .............   -  9 10
  70    To 1 Do .............   --  7  4
                                 ---------
                                 17  2
```
==

(103) 103 Peter JONES ....
```
1768    To 2 Taxes @ 9/10/d/ .   .. 19  8
  69    To 1 Do .............   .. 10  6
                                 ---------
                                 1 10  2
```

```
        Peter VINSON ........
1769    To 2 Taxes @ 10/6 ....   1  1            Rec/d/ ............. 1  8  4
  70    To 1 Do .............   ..  7  4         & Cost
                                 ---------
                                 1  8  4
```

```
        Phillip CAMBERLAIN
1770    To 3 Taxes @ 7/4 .....   1  2            1770  By Procl ........... 1  2
```

```
        Providence SHEPHERD
1770    To 1 Tax .............   .  7  4         1770  By Procl ........... . 7  4
```

```
        Precilla YEATES ......
1770    To 2 Taxes @ 7/4 .....   . 14  8        1770  By Procl. pr Son Job .. 14  8
```
==

(104) 104 Peter VANPELT ......
```
1770    To 1 Tax .............   .  7  4
```

```
        Richard BAKER ........
1768    To 8 Taxes @ 9/10 ....   3 18 10        V. .. By B: WYNNS Jur. ...  3 18 10
  69    To 7 Do .. @ 10/6 ....   3 13  6
```

(104) (Cont.)
```
 70    To 9 Do .. @ 7/4 .....    3  6            By Procl ..........  6 19  6
                                10 18  4                              10 18  4
```

```
       Robert PARKER ........
1768   To 1 Tax .............  ..  9 10
  69   To 1 Do .............  .. 10  6
  70   To 1 Do .............  ..  7  4
                                1  7  8
```

```
       Robert RODGERS .......
1768   To 6 Taxes @ 9/10/d/ . .2 19 60     BW    By B WYNNS Jur. .....  2 19 --
  69   To 6 Do .. @ 10/6 ....  .3  3
  70   To 8 Do .. @ 7/4 .....  2 18  8            By S: ROGERS Exr. ..  6  1  2
                               9  0? 82                                9  0  2
```

==

```
(105) 105 Rachael HAMBLETON
1768   To 2 Taxes @ 9/10/d/    .. 19  8
```

```
       Robert BRIDGERS ......
1768   To 2 Taxes @ 9/10/d/    .. 19  8
       To Cost warant .......      2  8         paid VANN
                                1  2  4
```

```
       Rachael REED mixt Blood
1768   To 1 Tax .............  ..  9 10
  69   To 1 Do .............  .  10  6
  70   To 2 Do .. @ 7/4 .....  .. 14  8
                                1  1=5
```

```
       Richard STAR .........
1768   To 1 Tax .............  ..  9 10
```

```
       Richard PARKER .......
1769   To 5 Taxes @ 10/6 ....  .2 12  6
  70   To 2 Do .. @ 7/4 .....  -- 14  8
                                3  7  2
```

==

```
(106) 106 Richard FELTON .....
1769   To 1 Tax .............  . 10  6
```

```
       Richard STALLINGS
1769   To 1 Tax .............  . 10  6
  70   To 1 Do .............  .  7  4
                               17 10
```

```
       Richard GREEN ........
1769   To 1 Tax .............  . 10  6
  70   To 1 Do .............  --  7  4
                               17 10
```

```
       Richard BAKER
1768   To 1 Tax .............  .  9 10           By prol. ..........  2  5  6
```

```
(106) (Cont.)
  69    To 2 Do @ 10/6 .......   1  1              Cost pd BIRD
  70    To 2 Do @ 7/4 ........  -- 14  8
                                 2  5  6
```

```
        Richard MATTHEWS
1768    To 1 Tax .............   9 10
```

```
(107) 107 Richchard NICHOLS
1768    To 1 Tax .............  . 9 10
```

```
        Rachael ROGERS .......
1768    To 1 Tax .............  . 9 10
```

```
        Richard TIMBERLAKE
1768    To 1 Tax .............  . 9 10
  69    To 2 Do @ 10/6 .......  1  1
                                1 10 10
```

```
        Robert EVANS .........
1768    To 2 Taxes @ 9/10/d/ .  .. 19  8       Rec/d/ .............  2 .. ..
  69    To 1 Do .............   .. 10  6       By Procl. ..........  . 4  8
  70    To 2 Do .. @ 7/4 .....  .. 14  8                             2  4  8
                                2  4 10
```

```
        Randolph GREEN
1768    To 2 Taxes @ 9/10/d/ .  .. 19  8
  69    To 1 Do .............   .. 10  6
                                1 11  2
```

```
(108) 108 Robert FAIRLESS
1768    To 1 Tax .............  . 9 10         By Lewis DEPREE ....  1  3  2
  69    To 2 Do @ 10/6 .......  1  1
                                1 10 10
```

```
        Robert SANDEFER ......
1769    To 1 Tax .............  . 10  6
```

```
        Robert TAYLOR
1769    To 1 Tax .............  . 10  6
```

```
        Robert CARR .........
1770    To 5 Taxes @ 7/4 .....  1 16  8     1770  By Procl. ..........  1 16  8
```

```
        Richard ANDREWS
1770    To 6 Taxes @ 7/4 .....  2  4           By prol pr BURCHET .  2  4
```

```
(109) 109 Richard YEATES .....
1770    To 3 Taxes @ 7/4/d/ ..  1  2           By prol. ..........  1  2  -
```

(109) (Cont.)

Sarah THOMSON

1768	To 1 Tax	.	9 10	V. .. By B. WYNNS Jur.	9 10
70	To 1 Do	.	7 4	By Procl	.	7 4
			17 2			17 2

Samuel WELLS ....

1768   To 2 Taxes @ 9/10/d/ .   .. 19 8   V. .. By B: WYNNS Jur. 19 8

Samuel WILLIAMS ......

1768   To 2 Taxes @ 9/10/d/ .   .. 19 8
69   To 2 Do .. @ 10/6 1   1
70   To 2 Do .. @ 7/4 .....   -- 14 8
                                  2 15 4

Solomon CRAWFORD .....

1768   To 1 Tax 9 10
69   To 1 Do ....   -- 10 6
70   To 1 Do ....   -- 7 4
                                    1 7 8

==

(110) 110 Samuel WILLIAMS Jun/r/.

1768   To 2 Taxes @ 9/10/d/ .   .. 19 8
69   To 2 Do .. @ 10/6   1   1
70   To 2 Do .. @ 7/4 .... 14 8
                                    1 15 4

Samuel TAYLOE ....

1768   To 1 Tax .... 9 10   By W M Rec/d/t 9 10
69   To 2 Do .. @ 10/6 ....   1 1   Rec/d/ 1 15 8
70   To 2 Do .. @ 7/4 .... 14 8   2 5 6
                                    2 5 6

Stephen SMITH ....

1768   To 1 Tax 9 10
69   To 1 Do 10 6
                                    1 0 4

Samuel EURE

1768   To 1 Tax 9 10
69   To 1 Do .... 10 6   Rec/d/ 1 7 8
70   To 1 Do ....   -- 7 4
                                    1 7 8

==

(111) 111 Solomon GREEN ......   Mind

1768   To 2 Taxes @ 9/10/d/ .   . 19 8
1770   To 2 Do .. @ 7/4 .....   -- 14 8
                                    1 14 4

Samuel TAYLOE ....

1768   To 1 Tax 9 10

---

(111) (Cont.)
      Samuel RABY ....
1768   To 1 Tax 9 10

      Stephen SMITH ....
1768   To 1 Tax 9 10

      Solomon KING ....
1768   To 5 Taxes @ 9/10/d/ . 2 9 2   V. .. By B. WYNNS Jur. ... 6 13 2
69   To 8 Do .. @ 10/6 .... 4 4   V.
                         6 13 2

==

(112) 112 Samuel EURE ....
1768   To 1 Tax 9 10

      Sarah ODOM ....
1768   To 4 Taxes @ 9/10/d/ . 1 19 4
69   To 4 Do .. @ 10/6 .... .2 2
70   To 6 Do .. @ 7/4 ..... .2 4
                         6 5 4

      Solomon GREEN ....
1768   To 2 Taxes @ 9/10/d/ . .. 19 8

      Stephen EURE ....
1768   To 4 Taxes @ 9/10/d/ . 1 19 4
69   To 5 Do .. @ 10/6 .... 2 12 6
70   To 6 Do .. @ 7/4 ..... 2 4
                         6 15 10   By Procl. 6 15 10

      Sarah SKINNER ....
1768   To51 Tax 9 10
69   To 1 Do 10 6
                         1 0 4

==

(113) 113 ~~Solomon~~/Stephen/ SHEPHERD
1768   To 3 Taxes @ 9/10/d/ . 1 9 6
69   To 3 Do .. @ 10/6 .... 1 11 6
70   To 4 Do .. @ 7/4 ..... 1 9 4   By Procl 4 10 4
                         4 10 4

      Sea?sbrook WILSON ....
1768   To 9 Taxes @ 9/10/d/ . 4 8 6
69   To 7 Do .. @ 10/6 .... 3 13 6
70   To 5 Do .. @ 7/4 ..... 1 16 8
                         9 18 8

      Stephen ROGERS ....
1768   To 3 Taxes @ 9/10 .... .1 9 6   V. .. By B. WYNNS Jur. 1 9 6
1770 To 4 Do .. @ 7/4 ..... .1 9 4   1770 By Procl 1 9 4
                         2 18 10   2 18 10

---

(113) (Cont.)
     Samuel BROWN ....
1769   To 1 Tax 10 6
  70   To 1 Do 7 4
                                  17 10

==

(114) 114 Stephen CROSS ......
1769   To 1 Tax .... 10 6   V.
  70   To 1 Do .... 7 4   V.   By B. WYNNS Jur. 17 10
                            17 10

     Sarah ===== ELLISS ...
1769   To 1 Tax 10 6
  70   To 1 Do 7 4
                            17 10

     Sarah WALTERS ....
1770   To 3 Taxes @ 7/4 ..... 1 2 -

     Sarah ELLISS Sn?r
1770   To 2 Taxes @ 7/4 .... 14 8   By prol 14 8

     Solomon HYOTT ....
1770   To 2 Taxes @ 7/4 .... 14 8

==

(115) 115 Simon TAYLOR ....
1768   To 1 Tax 9 10

     Samuel Bridger COLLINS
1768   To 3 Taxes @ 9/10/d/ . 1 9 6
6970 To 1 Do 7 4
                        1 16 10

     Suthey MANLEY ....
1768   To 1 Tax 9 10
  69   To 2 Do @ 10/6 .... 1 1
  70   To 2 Do @ 7/4 .... 14 8
                        2 5 6

     Samuel CRYER ....
1768   To 1 Tax 9 10
  70   To 3 Do @ 7/4 .... 1 2
                        1 11 10

     Samuel BROWN ....
1768   To 2 Taxes @ 9/10/d/ . .. 19 8
  69   To 2 Do .. @ 10/6 .... .1 1   Rec/d/ by J: DENTIN .. 2 .. 8

==

(116) 116 Samuel THOMAS ......
1768   To 1 Tax 9 10
  69   To 1 Do .... 10 6   By Jesse BIRD 1 7 8
  70   To 1 Do 7 4

(116) (Cont.)   1 7 8

Sarah KEEF ....
1768   To 1 Tax 9 10

Solomon WALKER ....
1768   To 2 Taxes @ 9/10/d/ . . 19 8

Solomon MANLEY ....
1768   To 2 Taxes @ 9/10/d/ . .. 19 8
70   To 2 Do .. @ 7/4 .... 14 8
                               1 14 4

Solomon WHITE ....
1768   To 1 Tax 9 10
69   To 1 Do 10 6
70   To 2 Do @ 7/4 ....   14 8   By Procl .... 1 15 --
                               1 15

==

(117) 117 Samuel BURRISH .....
17768 To 1 Tax 9 10
69   To 1 Do 10 6
70   To 1 Do 7 4
                               1 7 8

Stephen HALL ....
1768   To 2 Taxes @ 9/10/d/ . .. 19 8
69   To 2 Do .. @ 10/6 .... 1 1   By Procl 2 15 4
70   To 2 Do .. @ 7/4 ..... . 14 8
                             2 15 4

Simon VANPELT.
1768   To 1 Tax 9 10
69   To 2 Do @ 10/6 .... 1 1
                          1 10 10

Samuel POND ....
1769   To 1 Tax 10 6

==

(118) 118 Sarah WINBORN= .....
1769   To 7 Taxes @ 10/6 .... 3 13 6   Rec/d/. 3 13 6

Simon EVERITT Virg/a/.
1770   To 1 Tax 7 4

Sarah SCOTT ....
1770   To 6 Taxes @ 7/4 pd÷? 2 4   By prol 2 4

Samuel LEE ....
1770   To 6 Taxes @ 7/4/d/ .. 2 4   By prol .... 2 4 --

---

Simon WILLIAMS ....
1770   To 1 Tax .... -- 7 4   1770 By Procl 7 4

(118) (Cont.)
     Stephen LEE ....
1770   To 1 Tax .... -- 7 4   Rec/d/ 7 4
===

(119) 119 Samuel DAVIS ....
1770   To 2 Taxes @ 7/4 .... 14 8   Rec/d/ 14 8

     Sarah HOMES ....
1770   To 1 Tax 7 4

     Samuel PARKER
1770   To 1 Tax .... 7 4   Rec/d/ 7 4

     Solomon HOWARD
1770   To 2 Taxes @ 7/4 .... 14 8   Rec/d/ 14 8

     Solomon JONES
1770   To 2 Taxes @ 7/4 .... 14 8   Rec/d/ a ==== ...... (blank)
===

(120) 120 Stephen WILLIFORD
1770   To 1 Tax .... 7 4   Rec/d/ 7 4

     Sarah REILEY ....
1770   To 1 Tax 7 4

     Sarah MAYNOR.
1770   To 3 Taxes @ 7/4 ..... 1 2 --   By Procl .... 1 2 -
----

     Starkey SHARP ....
1770   To 6 Taxes @ 7/4 ..... 2 4   1770 By Procl 2 4

     Thomas FRYER ....
1768   To 2 Taxes @ 9/10/d/ . .. 19 8
  69   To 3 Do .. @ 10/6 .... 1 11 6
  70   To 3 Do .. @ 7/4 ..... 1 2 -
                        3 13 2
===

(121) 121 Thomas BAKER ....
1768   To 1 Tax 9 10

     Timothy MIZELL ....
1768   To 1 Tax .... 9 10   V. .. By B: WYNNS Jur 9 10
  69   To 1 Do 10 6
  70   To 2 Do .. @ 7/4 ..... . 14 8
                        1 15 -

     Thomas NORRISS ....
1768   To 1 Tax 9 10
  69   To 1 Do 10 6
  70   To 2 Do .. @ 7/4 ..... . 14 8
                .   1 15 -
----

(121) (Cont.)
```
        Trussay BETHA ........
1768    To 5 Taxes @ 9/10/d/ .   2  9  2       V. .. By B. WYNNS Jur. ...  2  9  2
69      To 5 Do .. @ 10/6 ....   2 12  6          By B WYNNS Junr Rec/t/  2 12  6
70      To 4 Do .. @ 7/4 .....   1  9  4          By Procl ..........     1  9  4
                                 6 11  -                                  6 11  -
```
===

(122) 122 Thomas BARNES
```
1768    To 5 Taxes @ 9/10/d/ .   2  9  2       BW
69      To 5 Do .. 10/6 ......   2 12  6       BW   By Benj/n/WYNNS Jur   5  1  8
                                 5  1  8
```

```
        Thomas HARRELL .......
1768    To 3 Taxes @ 9/10/d/ .   1  9  6       V. .. By B. WYNNS Jur ....  1  9  6
69      To 3 Do .. @ 10/6 ....   1 11  6
70      To 3 Do .. @ 7/4 .....   1  2             Rec/d/ .............    2 13  6
                                 4  3  -                                  4  3  -
```

```
        Thomas SPARKMAN
1768    To 2 Taxes a 9/10/d/ .   .. 19  8
69      To 2 Do .. @ 10/6 ....   1  1
70      To 3 Do .. @ 7/4 .....   1  2             Rec/d/ .............    3  2  8
                                 3  2  8
```

```
        Thomas RITTER ........
1768    To 2 Taxes @ 9/10/d/ .   .. 19  8
69      To 1 Do...............   -- 10  6
70      To 1 Do .............    ..  7  4
                                 1 17  6
```
===

(123) 123 Thomas PILAND
```
1768    To 3 Taxes @ 9/10/d/ .   .1  9  6      V.
69      To 3 Do .. @ 10/6 ....   =1 11  6      V.
70      To 3 Do .. @ 7/4 .....   1  2          V    By B. WYNNS Jur. ...  4  3 --
                                 4  3  -
```

```
        Thomas HARRELL the younger
1768    To 1 Tax .............   ..  9 10
69      To 1 Do...............   -- 10  6
70      To 1 Do .............    ..  7  4
                                 1  7 =8
```

```
        Thomas HARRELL Junr.
176870  To 3 Taxes @ 97/4 ....   1  2             Rec/d/ .............    1  2  -
```

```
        Thomas WINBORN .......
1770    To 1 Tax .............   ..  7  4
```

```
        Thomas BRITT Sen/r/ ...
1768    To 3 Taxes @ 9/10/ ...   1  9  6
```
===

(124) 124 Thomas DUNFORD
1768   To 1 Tax 9 10

        Thomas DAVIS ....
1768   To 1 Tax .... 9 10   By prol. Returnd ...   10
  69   To 1 Do .... 10 6   By prol. 10 4
                                   1 0 4   1 0 4

        Thomas SLADE ....
1768   To 1 Tax 9 10
  69   To 1 Do 10 6
  70   To 1 Do ....   7 4   By Procl 1 7 8
                                   1 7 8

        Thomas HOLLAMON
1768   To 1 Tax 9 10
  69   To 1 Do 10 6
  70   To 2 Do @ 7/4 .... -- 14 8
                                   1 15

        Thomas BOWSER ....
1768   To 2 Taxes @ 9/10/d/ . .. 19 8
  69.   To 3 Do .. @ 10/6 .... .1 11 6
                                   2 11 2

===

(125) 125 Thomas COTTON ......
1768   To 6 Taxes @ 9/10/d/ . 2 19 -
  69   To 7 Do .. @ 10/6 .... 3 13 6
  70   To 5 Do .. @ 7/4 ..... 1 16 8   1769 By Procl 3 2 8
  ..   8 9 2   By do. 5 6 6
                                                                        8 9 2

        Thomas ƐSORRILL?
1768   To 4 Taxes @ 9/10/d/.. 1 19 4   BW   By Benj/n/.WYNNS Jur. 1 19 4

        Thomas ARCHER ....
1768   To 4 Taxes @ 9/10/d/ . 1 19 4   By Colo. WYNNS 1 19 4
  70   To 5 Do .. @ 7/4 ..... 1 16 8   By Procl .... 1 16? 8
                                   3 16 -   3 16 -

        Thomas GILCREAS
1768   To 1 Tax ?............ .. 9 10
  70   To 1 Do 7 4
                                  17 2?

        Thomas WAINRIGHT
17689   To 1 Tax 10 6
===

(126) 126 Thomas BROWN ....
1769   To 1 Tax 10 6   1772
  70   To 1 Do ....   7 4   July 24/th/ By Benj:/n/ROBERTS . 17 10
                                  17 10

----

(126) (Cont.)

Thomas BOULTON ....
1769 To 1 Tax 10 6
70   To 1 Do ....   17 4   By Hardy MURFREE 17 10
                             17 10

Thomas BIRD ....
1769 To 1 Tax 10 6

Teagle RASCO ....   By prol. 10 6
(blank)

Thomas COPELAND ......
1769 To 5 Taxes @ 10/6 .... 2 12 6   By prol. 2 12 6
70   To 5 Do .. @ 7/4 ..... 1 16 8
                              4 9 2

==

(127) 127 Theophilus EVANS
1769 To 1 Tax 10 6
70   To 2 Do @ 7/4 .... 14 8
                              1 5 2   By Procl. 1 5 2

Thomas ENDICOTT over Seer C POLLOCK
1769 To 5 Taxes @ 10/6 .... 2 12 6

Thomas TOMKINS
1770 To 1 Tax 7 4

1770 Thomas EARLEY ....
      To 5 Taxes @ 7/4 ..... 1 16 8

Thomas WINBORN
1770 To 8 Taxes @ 7/4 ..... 2 18 8   1770 By prol. 2 18 8

==

(128) 128 Thomas HALL ....
1770 To 2 Taxes @ 7/4 .... 14 8

William VANN ....
1768 To 2 Taxes @ 9/10/d/ . .. 19 8   1768 Rec/d/. 19 8
69   To 2 Do .. @ 10/6 .... .1 1 -   BW   By B: WYNNS Jur. ... 1 1
70   To 4 Do .. @ 7/4 ..... 1 9 4   By Proc 1 9 4
                              3 10 -   3 10 -

William HAYSE ....
1768 To 1 Tax .... 9 10   V. .. By B. WYNNS Jur. 9 10
69   To 2 Do @ 10/6 .... 1 1
70   To 1 Do ....   -- 7 4
                              (blank)

William POWELL
1768 To 7 Taxes @ 9/10 .... 3 8 10   By prol 9 10 6
69   To 6 Do .. @ 10/6 .... 3 3
70   To 8 Do .. @ 7/4 ..... 2 18 8

```
(128) (Cont.)                    9  10   6
=========================================================================

(129) 129  William MATTHEWS ..
1768    To 1 Tax .............   ..  9 10
  69    To 1 Do .............   .. 10  6
  70    To 1 Do .............   ..  7  4
                                  1  7  8
-------------------------------------------------------------------------
        William WALTERS ......
1768    To 5 Taxes @ 9/10/d/ .   2  9 42
  69    To 4 Do .. @ 10/6 ....   2  2  -
  70    To 3 Do .. @ 7/4 .....   1  2
                                  5 13  2
-------------------------------------------------------------------------
        William WALTERS Jun/r/.
1768    To 4 Taxes @ 9/10/d/ .   1  9  6
  69    To 4 Do .. @ 10/6 ....   2  2
                                  3 11  6
-------------------------------------------------------------------------
        William DOUGHTIE
1768    To 3 Taxes @ 9/10/d/ .  .1  9  6
  69    To 2 Do .. @ 10/6 ....   1  1
  70    To 4 Do .. @ 7/4 .....  .1  9  4
                                  3 19 10
=========================================================================

(130) 130 William PARKER
1768    To 1 Tax .............   ..  9 10
  69    To 1 Do .............   .. 10  6
                                  1  -  4
-------------------------------------------------------------------------
        William THOMAS .......
1768    To 1 Tax .............   ..  9 10
  69    To 1 Do .............   .. 10  6
                                  1  -  4
-------------------------------------------------------------------------
        William DURNFORD.
1768    To 1 Tax .............   ..  9 10        V. .. By B. WYNNS Jur. ...  .  9 10
  69    To 1 Do .............   .. 10  6
  70    To 1 Do .............   ..  7  4
                                  1  7  8
-------------------------------------------------------------------------
        William GREEN
1768    To 3 Taxes @ 9/10/d/ .   1  9  6
  69    To 2 Do .. @ 10/6 ....   1  1
  70    To 1 Do .............   .  7  4
                                  2 17 10
=========================================================================

(131) 131 William FELTON
1768    To 3 Taxes @ 9/10/d/ .   1  9  6        V. .. By B. WYNNS Jur ....  1  9  6
  69    To 3 Do .. @ 10/6 ....   1 11  6
  70    To 3 Do .. @ 7/4 .....   1  2  -
                                  4  3
```

(131) (Cont.)

William COPELAND

1768	To 7 Taxes @ 9/10/d/ .	3 8 10	BW	By Benj? WYNNS Jur.	3 8 10
69	To 7 Do .. @ 10/6	3 13 6		By Procl	9̶6̶1̶3̶4̶8̶10
70	To 7 Do .. @ 7/4	2 11 4			9 13 8
		9 13 8			

William UMFLEET.

| 1768 | To 1 Tax .... | 9 10 | BW | By B: WYNNS Jur. ... . | 9 10 |

William ELLISS ....

1768	To 1 Tax	9 10
69	To 1 Do	10 6
70	To 1 Do	7 4
		1 7 8

===

(132) 132 William GATLING Jun/r/.

1768	To 2 Taxes @ 9/10/d/ .	. 19 8	BW		
69	To 3 Do .. @ 10/6	1 11 6	BW	By B: WYNNS	.2 11 2
70	To 4 Do .. @ 7/4	1 9 4	1770	By Procl.	1 9 4
		4 0 θ6			4 0 6

William GATLING Sen/r/.

1768	To 2 Taxes @ 9/10/d/ .	.. 19 8	BW		
69	To 2 Do .. @ 10/6	1 1 ..	B.W	By B: WYNNS Jur	2 - 8
70	To 2 Do .. @ 7/4	-- 14 8	1770	By prol	. 14 8
		2 15 4			2 15 4

William MORRISS ......

1768	To 1 Tax	9 10
69	To 2 Do @ 10/6	.1 1
70	To 1 Do	7 4
		1 18 2

William GOODMAN ......

1768	To 8 Taxes @ 9/10/d/ .	3 18 =8	BW		
69	To 7 Do .. @ 10/6	3 13 6	BW	By Benj/n/WYNNS Jur.	7 12 2
		7 12 2			

===

(133) 133 William ODOM ....

1768	To 2 Taxes @ 9/10/d/ .	.. 19 8	V. ..	By B. WYNNS Jur.	19 8
69	To 2 Do .. @ 10/6	1 1	69	By Procl.	1 1
70	To 1 Do	7 4	1770	By Procl	. 7 4
		2 8 -			2 8 -

Williss HUGHS ....

1768	To 2 Taxes @ 9/10/d/ .	.. 19 8
69	To 2 Do .. @ 10/6	1 1
		2 - 8

William EALLAN ....

| 1768 | To 1 Tax .... | .9 10 |

```
(133) (Cont.)
        William DAILDAY ......
1769    To 1 Tax ............. ..=10 =6
----------------------------------------------------------------------

        William BOYCE ........
1769    To 1 Tax ............. .. 10  6
 70     To 1 Do .............. ..  7  4         Rec/d/ in part ..... . 7  4
                               17 10
======================================================================

(134) 134 William ODAM of Ab/m/.
1769    To 1 Tax ............. . 10  6
 70     To 2 Do @ 7/4 ........ .. 14  8         1770  By Procl ........... . 7  4
                                1  5  2
----------------------------------------------------------------------

        William VANN Jun/r/
1770    To 1 Tax ............. -  7  4
----------------------------------------------------------------------

        William CRAFFORD .....
1770    To 1 Tax ............. --  7  4
----------------------------------------------------------------------

        William RITTER Jun/r/.
1770    To 1 Tax ............. -  7  4          Rec/d/ ............. . 7  4
----------------------------------------------------------------------

        William M/C/ CONE Sen/r/
17698   To 3 Taxes @ 9/10/d/ . 1  9  6
======================================================================

(135) 135 William HOBBS ......                  Rec/d/ ............. . . 8
1768    To 4 Taxes @ 9/10/d/ . 1 19  4          Rec/d/ ............. 1  8
        To Cost worant ....... _2__8            Rec/d/ ............. . 13  4
                                2  2                                 2  2 =0
----------------------------------------------------------------------

        William WILLIAMS
1768    To 1 Tax ............. . 9 10
 69     To 1 Do .............. . 10  6
 70     To 1 Do .............. .. .7  4
                                1  7  8
----------------------------------------------------------------------

        William BARNES .......
1768    To 1 Tax ............. . 9 10           By Procl ........... . 9 10
----------------------------------------------------------------------

        William BOON
1768    To 2 Taxes @ 9/10/d/ . .. 19  8
----------------------------------------------------------------------

        West MOSELY mind
1768    To 1 Tax ............. . .9 10
 69     To 1 Do .............. . 10  6
                                1  0  4
======================================================================

(136) 136 William PORTER .....
1768    To 5 Taxes @ 9/10/d/ . 2  9  2
 69     To 5 Do .. @ 10/6 .... 2 12  6
 70     To 6 Do .. @ 7/4 ..... 2  4_            Rec/d/ ............. 7  5  8
```

62

William MURFREE
1768	To 8 Taxes @ 9/10/d/ .	3 18 10
69	To 8 Do .. @ 10/6	4 4
70	To 7 Do .. @ 7/4	2 11 4
		10 14 2

William KNIGHT ....
1768	To 4 Taxes @ 9/10/d/ .	1 19 4
69	To 2 Do Pat/r/. @ 10/6	1 1
70	To 3 Do .. @ 7/4	1 2
		4 2 4

William VAUGHN
1768	To 3 Taxes @ 9/10/d/ .	1 9 6	Rec/d/ in part ..... 1 =4 3
69	To 3 Do .. @ 10/6	1 11 6	Rec/d/ 2 18 9
70	To 3 Do .. @ 7/4	1 2	4 3
		4 3	

==

(137) 137 William DRIVER
1768	To 9 Taxes @ 9/10/d/ .	4 8 6	Rec/d/ by Colo.. WYNNS 12 16 4
69	To 9 Do .. @ 10/6 .	4 14 6	
70	To 10 Do .. @ 7/4	3 13 4	
		12 16 4	

William BIRDE Sen/r/.
1768	To 3 Taxes @ 9/10/d/ .	1 9 6	By Procl. 3 5 2
69	To 2 Do .. @ 10/6	1 1	
70	To 2 Do .. @ 7/4	.1 14 8	
		3 5 2	

William HORTON ....
1768	To 1 Tax	.. 9 10	
69	To 1 Do	.. 10 6	Rec/d/. by Jesse BIYRD . 7 ..
70	To 1 Do	.. 7 4	
		1 7 8	

William FREEMAN
1768	To 2 Taxes @ 9/10/d/ .	19 8	
69	To 1 Do Cons/t/.	. 10 6	By Procl &Cost 1 10 4
70	To 2 Do .. @ 7/4	. 14 8	
		2 4 10?	

==

(138) 138 William LEADOM
| 1768 | To 2 Taxes @ 9/10/d/ | . 19 8 |

William CLARKE ....
1768	To 1 Tax	. 9 10
69	To 1 Do	. 10 6
		1 0 4

(138) (Cont.)
```
            William PEELE ........
1768    To 2 Taxes @ 9/10 ....      19  8
  69    To 2 Do .. @ 10/6 ....   1   1
  70    To 2 Do .. @ 7/4 .....   .. 14  8
                                 2  16  4
```

```
            Williss NICHOLS ......
1768    To 4 Taxes @ 9/10/d/ .   1 19  4        Rec/d/ ............   3..10.10
  69    To 3 Do .. @ 10/6 ....   1 11  6
                                 3 10 10
```

```
            William EARLY ........
1768    To 7 Taxes @ 9/10/d/ .   3  8 10        By Procl ..........  3  8 10
```
===

(139) 139 Williss NICHOLS Jun/r/.
```
1768    To 1 Tax .............   .  9 10
```

```
            William COTTON .......
1768    To 2 Taxes @ 9/10 ....   .. 19  8
```

```
            William TOMSON
1768    To 3 Taxes @ 9/10 ....   1  9  6
  70    To 2 Do .. @ 7/4 .....      14  8       By Procl ...........  2  4  2
                                 2  4  2
```

```
            William JENKINS ......
1768    To 1 Tax .............   .  9 10
  69    To 1 Do ..............   .  10  6       By prol. ...........  1  -  4
                                 1  0  4
```

```
            Whitaker REEDD .......
1768    To 1 Tax .............   .  9 10
  69    To 1 Do ..............   .. 10  6
  70    To 1 Do ..............   ..  7  4
                                 1  7  8
```
===

(140) 140 William ASKEW ......
```
1768    To 1 Tax .............   .  9 10    BW   By B. WYNNS Jur .... .. 9 10
  69    To 1 Do ..............   .. 10  6        By Procl. ..........  1 12  6
  70    To 3 Do @ 7/4 ........   1  2                                  2  2  4
                                 2  2  4
```

```
            William DAWS .........
1768    To 2 Taxes @ 9/10/d/ .   .. 19  8
  69    To 2 Do .. @ 10/6 ....   1   1
  70    To 2 Do .. @ 7/4 .....   .. 14  8
                                 2 15  4
```

```
            William LASSITER
1768    To 12 Taxes @ 9/10/d/    5 18
  69    To 9 Do .. @ 10/6 ....   4 14  6         By prol. ........... 12 16 :6
  70    To 6 Do .. @ 7/4 .....   2  4
```

(140) (Cont.)   12 16 6

  William MACKEY ....
1768 To 3 Taxes @ 9/10/d/ . 1 9 6

===

(141) 141 William EVANS ......
176998 To 3 Taxes @ 9/10/d/ . 1 9 6   By Capt. SUMNER .... 4 3 ..
 69 To 3 Do .. @ 10/6 .... 1 11 6   By Cost 2 8
 70 To 3 Do .. @ 7/4 ..... 1 2   4 5 8
             4 3
   To Cost 2 8
             4 5 8

  William LOYD ....
1768 To 1 Tax 9 10
 69 To 1 Do .... 10 6   By Procl 1 7 8
 70 To 1 Do 7 4
             1 7 8

  Williss HARE ....
1768 To 1 Tax 9 10
 69 To 1 Do .... 10 6   By Procl 1 7 8
 70 To 1 Do 7 4
             1 7 8

  William MORGHAN
1768 To 2 Taxes @ 9/10/d/ . .. 19 8
 69 To 3 Do .. @ 10/6 .... 1 11 6   By Procl 4 0 6
 70 To 4 Do .. @ 7/4 ..... 1 9 4
             4 0 6

===

(142) 142 William TRADER
1769 To 1 Tax 10 6
 70 To 1 Do .... 7 4   By prl 17 10
             17 10

  William THORL ....
1769 To 2 Taxes @ 10/6 .... 1 1   Rec/d/. .... 1 1 -

  William DAUGHTRY .....
1769 To 6 Taxes .. @ 10/6 . 3 3
 70 To 6 Do .. @ 7/4 ..... 2 4
             5 7

  William TAYLOR ....
1769 To 2 Taxes .. @ 10/6 . 1 1
 70 To 2 Do .. @ 7/4 ..... . 14 8
             1 15 8

  William BARDEN ....
1769 To 2 Taxes @ 10/6 .... 1 1
 70 To 1 Do .... 7 4   By Procl 1 8 4
             1 8 4

(143) 143 William BALEY
1769 To 2 Taxes .. @ 10/6 . 1 1
  70 To 3 D̲o̲ .. @ 7/4 ..... 1 2   By prol. Rec/d/ .... 2 3 ..
                              2 3

     William FIGURES ......
1769 To 4 Taxes .. @ 10/6 . 2 2
  70 To 4 D̲o̲ .. @ 7/4 ..... 1 9 4   By prol. 3 11 4
                              3 11 4

     William DAVIDSON
1769 To 1 Tax 10 6

     WalterB̲L̲A̲K̲E̲ Cons/t/.
1769 To 1 Tax 10 6
  70 To 1 D̲o̲ 7 4
                              17 10

     Williss WELLS ....
1769 To 1 Tax 10 6

==

(144) 144 William MOORE ......
1769 To 1 Tax 10 6

     William MULLEN ....
1770 To 2 Taxes @ 7/4 ..... . 14 8   1770 By Procl. 14 8

     William CRICHELOW
1770 To 1 Tax.... 7/4 ..... . ̶1̶0̶7̶ 64

     William RAY ....
1770 To 1 Tax 7 4

     William BRITT ....
1770 To 1 Tax 7 4

     William CARTER
1770 To 2 Taxes @ 7/4 ..... . 14 8   Rec/d/. 14 8

==

(145) 145 William GRIFFITH ...
1770 To 4 Taxes @ 7/4 ..... 1 9 4   Rec/d/. 1 95 4

     William BIRD Jun/r/
1770 To 1 Tax 7 4

     William CONNER ....
1770 To 2 Taxes @ 7/4 .... 14 8   1770 By Procl. 14 8

     William WEVER ....
1770 To 2 Taxes @ 7/4 .... 14 8   By Procl 14 8

     William WALKER ....
1770 To 1 Tax .... 7 4   By prol .... - 7 4

66

```
(145) (Cont.)
       William KELLEY .......
1770    To 2 Taxes @ 7/4 ..... .. 14  8
=================================================================================

(146) 146 Williss GODWIN .....
1770    To 1 Tax ............. .  7  4          By Jesse BIRD ...... .  7  4
---------------------------------------------------------------------------------
       William BROWN ........
1770    To 4 Taxes @ 97/±04/d/  1 09  4         By Procl ........... 1  9  4
---------------------------------------------------------------------------------
       William B KIPPAX
1770    To 3 Taxes @ 7/4 .....  1  2
---------------------------------------------------------------------------------
       William LASSITER Jun/r/
1770    To 7 Taxes @ 7/4/d/ ..  2 11  4         By prol. ........... 2 11  4
---------------------------------------------------------------------------------
       Zadock BAKER
1770    To 4 Taxes @ 7/4 .....  1  9  4
=================================================================================

(147) 147 Mary CRICHELOW .....
1770    To 1 Tax ...7/4/d/ ... . 97±04          Rec/d/ ............. .  7  4
---------------------------------------------------------------------------------
       Matthew REVILL .......
1770    To 1 Tax ............. .  7  4     1770 By Procl ........... .  7  4
---------------------------------------------------------------------------------
       Matthew TURNER Cons/t/.
1770    To 1 Tax ............. .  7  4
---------------------------------------------------------------------------------
       Matthew HASTEY
1770    To 1 Tax ............. .  7  4          By prol. ........... .  7  4
---------------------------------------------------------------------------------
       Mary ARCHER .........
1770    To 2 Taxes @ 7/4/d/ .  .. 14  8
=================================================================================

(148) 148 Matthew BECK
1770    To 1 Tax ............. .  7  4
---------------------------------------------------------------------------------
       Nicholas BOON ........
1770    To 4 Taxes @ 7/4/d/ ..  1  9  4
---------------------------------------------------------------------------------
       Nicholas PERRY .......
1770    To 7 Taxes @ 7/4 .....  2 11  4         By Procl .............2 11  4
---------------------------------------------------------------------------------
       Nathaniel OVERNTON ...
1770    To 1 Tax ............. .  7  4          Rec/d/ ............. .  7  4
---------------------------------------------------------------------------------
       Nicholas ASKEW
1770    To 6 Taxes @ 7/4 .....  2  4      1770 By Procl .......... 2  4
=================================================================================

(149) 149 Nehemiah MILLER
1770    To 1 Tax ............. .  7  4     [Remainder of page is blank.]
```

(150) [Page not numbered.]
Recd. of parsons not lested for the year 1770
                                Rec/d/. 3 Taxes Hugh HORTEN 1:2:6?
[Remainder of page is blank.]
===

(151) [Page not numbered.]
Rec/d/. by Henry DILDAY Ju/r/ 17/10 for 1769.
1770 [End of entry.]
[Remainder of page is blank.]
===

END OF BOOK

FEMALE GIVEN NAMES
(Cont.)
Jane WILLIAMS
(Cont.) 52
Jemima REED 40
Jernett COTTON
88
Keziah DOUGLIS
90
Martha HARE 96
Martha HOLLAMON
97
Mary ARCHER 147
Mary CRICHELOW
147
Mary FELTON 93
Mary HARE 96
Mary VANN 96
Nanny FLOOD 100
Patience WARRIN
102
Precilla YEATES
103
Providence
SHEPHERD 103
Rachael
HAMBLETON 105
Rachael REED
105
Rachael ROGERS
107
Sarah ELLISS
114
Sarah ELLISS,
Sr. 114
Sarah HOMES 119
Sarah KEEF 116
Sarah MAYNOR
120
Sarah ODOM 112
Sarah REILEY
120
Sarah SCOTT 118
Sarah SKINNER
112
Sarah THOMSON
109
Sarah WALTERS
114
Sarah WINBORN
118
Suthey MANLEY
115
Trussay BETHA
121
FENDLEY
Benjamin 8
FIGG
Joseph 37
FIGURES
William 143
FLEMMON
John 74
FLOOD
Jesse 84
Nanny 100
FLUDD
Absalom 5
FORSETT
David 21
FREEMAN
Amos 7
Jacob 64
William 137
FRYER
Isaac 45
Jacob 48
James 59
Jonathan 44
Thomas 120

-G-

GATLING
Edward 25
Edwd., Jr. 25
George 28
John 51
William, Jr.
132
William, Sr.

GATLING (Cont.)
William, Sr.
(Cont.) 132
GAY
James 81
GILBERT
John 83
GILCREAS
Thomas 125
GODWIN
Barneby 8
Kirney 90
Williss 146
GOODMAN
Joel 50
William 132
GOODMON
Henry 31
GREEN
John, Jr. 42
Joseph 72
Malichi 98
Matthias 95
Randolph 107
Richard 106
Solomon 111,112
William 130
GRIFFIN
Joseph 37,54
GRIFFITH
Hannah 33
William 145
GWIN
Asa 3

-H-

HAILE
James 77
Jesse 78
HALL
Absalom 6
Isaac 75
Stephen 117
Thomas 128
HAMBLETON
John 53
Rachael 105
HANCOCK
David 19
HARE
Edward 23
John 17,68,86
Luke 92
Martha 96
Mary 96
Mosses 95
William 141
HARGROVES
Nathaniel 100
HARRELL
Aaron 1
Adam 7
Charles 12
David 18
Demsey 18
Jesse 48,56
Jethro 52
John 51
Josiah 51
Peter 102
Thomas 122
Thomas, Jr. 123
Thomas, the
younger 123
HARRISS
James 64
HARROLD
Elijah 24
HASTEY
Matthew 147
HAYSE
Jacob 35,80
James 35
William 128
HEDGSPETH
Charles 12
James 63,88
HILL
_____ 76
Henry 33

HILL (Cont.)
Isaac 72
Michael 98
HINES (See also
HYNES)
John 46
HINTON
Aaron 4
Amos 5
HOBBS
Barneby 11
Joseph 74
William 135
HOGGARD
John 78
HOLLAMON
Aaron 8
Edmund 24
Martha 97
Thomas 124
HOLLAWAY
Absalom 4
HOMES
Hamer 34
Sarah 119
HOOKER
James 89
HORTEN
Hugh 150
HORTON
David 19
Hugh 33
William 137
HOWARD
Edward 25
Elijah 26
James, Sr. 77
Solomon 119
HUBBARD
John 61
HUGHS
Williss 133
HYNES (See also
HINES)
Mosses 94
HYOTT
Solomon 114

-I-

IRELAND
Grafton 29

-J-

JENKINS
Charles, Jr. 15
William 139
Wm. 71
JONES
Abram 7
Charles 13
Hardy 32
James 60,72
Jesse 44
Joseph 84
Peter 103
Solomon 119

-K-

KEEF
Sarah 116
KEEFE
Epheriam 26
KEEL
Jacob 88
KELLEY
William 145
KING
Henry 32
Henry, Jr. 32
Nehemiah 100
Nicholas 99
Solomon 111
KIPPAX
William B. 146
KITTRELL
John 34
Mosses 97
KNIGHT

KNIGHT (Cont.)
Demsey 21
Nehemiah 101
William 136

-L-

LANDING
James 45
LANG
James 50
John 55
Joshua 43
LANGSTON
Josiah 46
Luke 92
Mosses 95
LASSITER
Jonas 70
William 140
William, Jr.
146
LEADOM
Elizabeth 25
William 138
LEE
John 58
Levey 91
Samuel 118
Stephen 118
LEVEY
Alexander 7
LEWIS
Isaac 69
John 55
LINCH
Elizabeth 22
LITTLE
Geo. 13
George 30
LIVERMON
John 66
LOYD
William 141
LUCAS
James 53

-M-

M.
W. 80,110
MABRY
Wm. 10
MC CONE
John 56
William, Sr.
134
MC GLOHON
James 65
MC SIMONS
Humphry 33
MACKEY
William 140
MAINER (See also
MAYNOR)
Aaron 2
MANEY
J. 58
James 58
MANLEY
Abel 5
Gabriel 30
Littleton 92
Mosses 98
Solomon 116
Suthey 115
MARTIN
Christopher 15
MATTHEWS
Andrew 1
Anthony 3
Josiah 38
Richard 106
William 129
MAUDLING
Demsey 19
MAYNOR (See also
MAINER)
John 71
Sarah 120
MELTIAH

MELTIAH (Cont.)
Josiah 81
MERITT
John 84
MICHENER
Jeremiah 63
MILLER
Nehemiah 149
MIXED BLOOD
BOON, James 55
REED, Rachael
105
MIZELL
Timothy 121
MONTGOMERY
John 58
MOORE
Benton 8
John, Sr. 62
Joseph 76
Mosses 99
Shadrick 99
William 144
MORGAN
Hardy 31
MORGHAN
William 141
MORRISS
Benjamin 8
John 55
Nathan 101
William 132
MOSELY
West 135
MOTT
John 61
MULATTOES
REED, Jemima 40
MULLEN
William 144
MURFREE
H. 71
Hardy 126
James 83
William 136

-N-

NEWSOM
Hosea 34
NICHOLS
Richard 107
Williss 138
Williss, Jr.
139
NICKENS
Carter 14
James 66
NORFLEET
Joseph 42
NORRISS
Thomas 121
NORTHCOTT
John 65
NORVILLE
Benjamin 10
NOWELL
Demsey 21
James 71

-O-

OCCUPATION
Overseer 99,127
ODAM
Abm. 134
Demsey 18
Jacob 56
John 47
William 134
ODOM
Aaron 3
Sarah 112
William 133
OLEVENT
Jesse 42
OSMUNT (See also
OYZMOND)
Francis 27
OUTLAW
James 80

70

www.ingramcontent.com/pod-product-compliance
Lightning Source LLC
Chambersburg PA
CBHW031133020426
42333CB00012B/359